T0042212

STARTING FROM SCRATCH

Andrea Marcolongo

STARTING FROM SCRATCH
The Life-Changing Lessons of Aeneas

Translated from the Italian
by Will Schutt

Europa
editions

Europa Editions
1 Penn Plaza, Suite 6282
New York, N.Y. 10019
www.europaeditions.com
info@europaeditions.com

Translation by Will Schutt
Original title: *La lezione di Enea*
Translation copyright © 2022 by Europa Editions

Library of Congress Cataloging in Publication Data is available
ISBN 978-1-60945-749-5

Marcolongo, Andrea
Starting from Scratch

Art direction by Emanuele Ragnisco
instagram.com/emanueleragnisco

Cover image by Roman Tiraspolsky / Alamy Stock Photo

Prepress by Grafica Punto Print – Rome

Printed in the USA

CONTENTS

To My Country, Italy

STARTING FROM SCRATCH

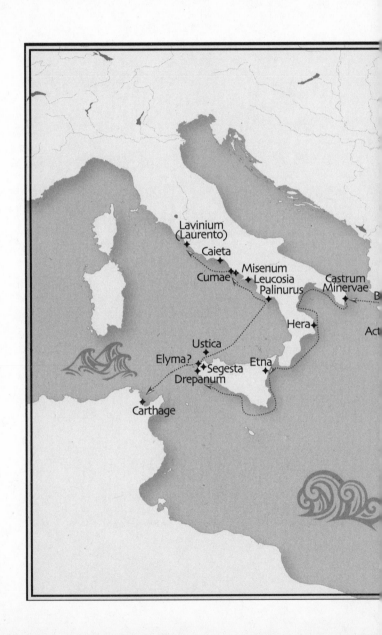

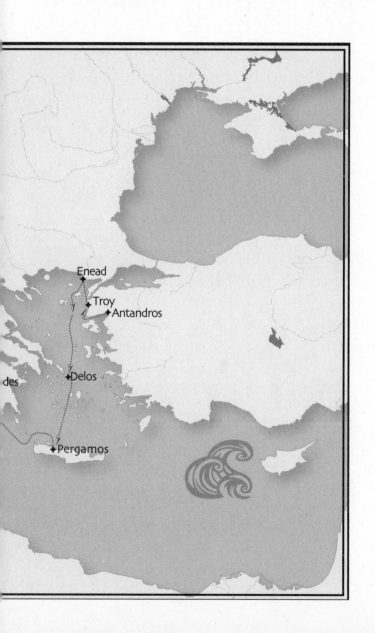

THE LESSON OF AENEAS

Learn valor from me, my son, and true toil;
fortune from others.
(*Aeneid*, 12.435-436)

I have never heard anyone, when asked to name their favorite hero, answer Aeneas. And that's coming from someone who lived for a time in Rome.

If people have an impression of Aeneas, even a faint one, which is not a given, since more often than not people have nothing to say about him—they greet him with total indifference—it's that he's a cad. Fate's errand boy, with a mushy spine. Someone tossed about by the gods who stumbles upon an empire almost by accident. Someone who runs for the hills whenever something really epic happens to him, like being seduced by an irresistible queen from Carthage eager to offer him her kingdom. After all, what kind of hero wanders around the Mediterranean with his hands clasped and can only psych himself up with *pietas*?

I have long asked myself why the character of Aeneas has had to endure such harsh judgments, judgments that would have us believe that the *Aeneid* is a story for the faint of heart. It only recently dawned on me that the mix of discomfort and irritation that people feel when reading Virgil's epic—or at the mere mention of it—is connected not to the shabby figure of Aeneas so much as to the historical moment in which one reads the *Aeneid.* And to my "recently" above, I feel compelled to add "unfortunately."

The *Aeneid* is not an epic for times of peace. Its verses are not suited to smooth sailing. When all is well, the *Aeneid* bores people to death—and lucky are those who, for centuries, have had the luxury of yawning at its hexameters. Woe is us, for the song of the *Aeneid* is meant for moments when people desperately need to wrap their heads around an *after* that is shockingly different from the *before* they'd always known. In the parlance of forecasters: The *Aeneid* is warmly recommended reading for days when you're in the eye of a storm without an umbrella. On sunny days, it serves little to no purpose.

That's how things have stood from the start, after all. From before the start, actually. Virgil was writing about Aeneas's travails while he himself was treading water during that historic age when the Roman Empire was rearing its head over the rubble of the Republic.

The *Aeneid* came back in vogue in the Middle Ages, when no one knew which way to turn or whose side to take or what language to speak after the fall of the Roman Empire in the West, and Odoacer deposed Romulus Augustus with a chuck under the chin. It did so again in Dante's Florence, a city divided like cells into Guelphs and

Ghibellines, Blacks and Whites, and would have to wait a century for the arrival of Lorenzo the Magnificent. People also turned to Virgil at the turn of the twentieth century, when the world was suspended between euphoria over the dawn of modernity and terror upon quickly discovering modernity's side effects: Being "new" is always a terrible burden.

That is to say nothing of the birth of Christ, the great before-and-after event that divided human history into two distinct parts. For a long time, humanity tried to find evidence of the new Christian era in Virgil's verses, twisting them out of shape in order to substantiate something that, by its divine nature, could not possibly be substantiated— and that unsettled people for its lack of precedence.

That's natural. In times of peace and prosperity we ask Homer to teach us about life. We understandably demand to dwell in something other than dead calm. Our *thymos*, as the Greek philosophers called it, otherwise known as élan, our hunger for life, gallops ahead at breathtaking speed— and if we really are guided, deep down, by the winged charioteer that Plato describes in the *Phaedrus*, it is clearly the black horse of passion now pulling our chariot, and the white horse of reason is perfectly happy to bide its time.

Yet whenever there is historic upheaval, we set the *Iliad* and *Odyssey* down on the nightstand and snatch the *Aeneid* off our shelves. All we feel is fear and the desperate need to survive—our invisible charioteer no longer worries about where to go but how to get the wagon back on its wheels after it has toppled over and crippled both horses.

Why didn't anyone tell us this about the *Aeneid*? Obviously, in times of war, nobody is assembling fancy critical editions. And in times of peace people just want to move on, to forget.

* * *

Sitting on the banks, waiting for our enemies' bodies to float by, we are well within our rights to indulge in the luxury of choosing to side with Hector or Achilles, or of browsing the menu of Ulysses' adventures, and his women. But when we have to fight to ensure that the body drifting downstream is not our own, that is when Aeneas is called for. So why, even as we recognize how much we need him, can we not help but detest him, at least a little? Because Virgil's hero does nothing to comfort us. On the contrary. He has the nerve to provoke us.

The *Aeneid* opens with Troy in ruins—and does everything to demolish all we think it is we want and feel while we're surrounded by ruins ourselves. Fear, for starters. Aeneas suffers, his every action is imbued with pain, yet he seems immune to anguish. Where we remain—understandably—petrified, he presses on and never stops marching forward.

As we shall see, he cries a lot. Yet he always answers fear with courage. He doesn't shirk his duty to look spine-tingling reality in the face. He doesn't hesitate to name what moments ago no one had a name for or confront phenomena no one had ever experienced before.

Aeneas thinks, takes stock, struggles to make sense of things. With the rigor of rationality, he creates order out of chaos. That's exactly why Aeneas seems so detestable at first. Like us, he doesn't know what to do, yet still he does it. Like us, he doesn't know where to begin, but when in doubt he begins. He's irritating, true—because he keeps reminding us that it is fundamental to go on.

What's more, Aeneas doesn't correspond to our idea of a strongman (criticize him all you like, but the inverse of Aeneas is a dictator). He is anything but the proverbial man at the top, in whose hands the weight of founding a nation is placed so that we may wash our own of the endeavor.

Aeneas commands nothing if not a handful of fellow ne'er-do-wells. He's not even that tough: All he does is fumble about on his voyage from Troy to Latium. And he doesn't embark on his voyage alone; he travels with his father and son in tow and the Penates in his pocket. If only he had a weapon or a magic potion or a superpower that distinguished him from ordinary survivors like us—something that kept us from having to conclude that, if he can do it, so can we.

Being Aeneas means one thing: answering destruction with reconstruction. That's the lesson of Aeneas.

1
How This Book Came to Be

Everything holds on—
everything goes on—
everything subsists—
everything resists—
—Giorgio Manganelli, from *Appendix IIA, Poems*

The truth is I didn't want to write this book. I would have preferred to go on being confused and ambivalent about Virgil, unsure whether I liked the epic or whether it bored me stiff. Maybe I would have preferred to go on opening the *Aeneid* out of curiosity every three or four years, the way I had since my school days—jotting down in my notebooks what I didn't get about the poem and postponing the obligation to understand it.

At one point I even gave Virgil a serious go, with real determination. At the time I only managed to scrape together random notes, flimsy insight, perhaps to work out in a book project at some point, but I put it off so long that I wound up forgetting all about it. I wasn't in a rush.

Then, in December 2019, as I was packing up to move from Rome to Paris, I stumbled across the notebooks. I opened them, curious to contemplate what I had once been like from the shores of what I had become. I was amazed to note that I had begun investigating the meaning of the *Aeneid* long before cataloging my very personal reasons for loving Greek. Especially galling was taking note of my failure. After years of study, I was further behind than when I had started, and I had to admit that I still hadn't understood a thing about Virgil's epic. Rather than blame myself or feel moved to dig deeper, I felt pleased by my shallowness and began mocking Virgil—as people have done for ages.

In my defense, we now live in an era of far different magnitude, so back then I didn't have the time it would take to fathom the *Aeneid*, and up until 2020 it would have no doubt seemed crazy to shut myself in the house to attempt to; that wasn't my plan. It should also be said that I was perfectly happy to go on living without having grasped its meaning; such a goal was at the bottom of my to-do list—down there with reading the Vedas in their entirety, improving my Spanish, learning to dance—because I knew that I would probably never get around to it, caught up as I was in the collective hubris that had me racing about and being productive and parading around and traveling and doing this and undoing that. Besides, no one was clamoring to be told the meaning of the *Aeneid*. Much less demanding that I be the one to tell them. For centuries the world was doing just fine without Virgil and Aeneas. We were all doing just fine.

On one of my last days in Rome, I took that notebook-cum-keepsake to my editor, to laugh about the ones that got away and the books that never got written. "What if I wrote a book," I hazarded, "about why we should hate Aeneas?" Shortly after, my need for Aeneas materialized. Some will say it was karma, but I prefer to call it a wake-up call.

Nowhere was it written that we would wake up every morning to find that the world into which we were born and in which we have always lived was still the same, let alone better.

But that's what we believed, and we comforted each other with that thought.

Aeneas is not the type of hero that one fine day climbs out of the schoolbooks and plants himself firmly in the popular imagination. He's no Achilles, who serves as the archetype of our every outburst. Nor is he a Ulysses, whom we can pull out of our back pocket to justify our hunger for adventure. Least of all is the *Aeneid* the kind of book to keep on the nightstand to accompany our wildest dreams— usually it lies forgotten on the top shelf of our bookcase, alongside the books we will never re-read but, out of super- stition, don't dare give away.

We come across Aeneas by chance. We bump into him as he's passing by—if we are not already on our knees. We collide with Virgil whenever our world, the world we thought would stay the same forever, has gone to pieces. And we with it. So, even if I had known the epic since my school days, and had studied Virgil in college, I didn't officially run up against the *Aeneid* until early March 2020, while sheltering in place.

It sounds strange to say that—it sounds strange to me most of all, as I write this. But that was when I first encoun- tered Aeneas.

* * *

In an article titled *"Noi, Enea,"* which appeared in the magazine *La fiera letteraria* in 1949, the poet Giorgio Caproni writes:

> I have visited many Italian cities, but I never met Aeneas anyplace else. At least I did not encounter the one plausible Aeneas, the one Aeneas truly alive in all his solitude and humanity. The one Aeneas, that is, deserving of a monument in the middle of a square, the one symbol of modern human-ity, in this age when man is truly alone on the earth, bearing the weight of a tradition on his shoulders, which he is trying to sustain even though that same tradition no longer sustains him, in his hand a hope that is still too small and unsteady to lean on, which he must, nevertheless, carry to safety.

Caproni is referring to a small monument to Aeneas that sits in Genoa's Piazza Bandiera, a work by Francesco Baratta (1726). It's one of the rare statues in Italy dedicated to the Trojan hero. That alone speaks volumes about the mix of forgetfulness and irritation that Virgil has always had to endure among Italians—seeing as Aeneas founded Italy *ex novo*, according to the *Aeneid*.

Gazing up at this monument of the exhausted exile trudging forward with his father over his shoulder and his son's hand in his, Caproni decided to gather three poems about the prostration of postwar Italy into a book called *The Passage of Aeneas* (1956). And it was reread-ing the above passage—and finally getting it in spite of myself—that the *Aeneid* suddenly became indispensable to me. So much so that there were days at the height of the pandemic when I wondered how I could have ever done without it.

Because in the meantime we had suddenly become that same modern humanity trudging forward over the ruins. That was when, like Caproni, I "encountered" the one plausible Aeneas "in all his solitude and humanity."

While the world around me was trying to sustain a lifestyle that it could no longer sustain, and hope was still too flimsy to make plans or predictions about the future, I began to perceive the meaning of the *Aeneid* that had long escaped my grasp. And with that discovery came the need to write about it.

I called my editor again, no longer daring to laugh at Virgil's expense—in fact, there were times reading the *Aeneid* that I now wept. That's how this book came to be.

* * *

Good Queen, by your command I will relive
unspeakable woe, and tell of how the Greeks
destroyed the doomed kingdom of mighty Troy,
and all the misery I saw and played a part in.
(*Aeneid,* 2.3-6)

It isn't hard for me to see that my words might seem dramatic. My intention with this book is not to do as Dido does in the lines above and *renovare dolorem*, to borrow Virgil's words, which have become shorthand for someone who enjoys throwing salt on the wound.

For my part, I am aware that very few people today still remember having had to slog through the *Aeneid* at school. Because no one remembers ever having studied it. Yet we have all suffered—in no small way—from boredom while trying to follow the plot or feelings of despondency as we attempted to recite its hexameters. But—by some miracle!—we forgot about the *Aeneid* the minute we reached the last page, as if we'd dunked our heads in the River Lethe.

Virgil's epic is in fact portentous, its content disappearing as soon as we have closed our schoolbooks, leaving in its place the more mysterious—but without a doubt most enduring—example of the blank slate theory. No need to make excuses. It would be cowardly to try to defend ourselves by dashing off justifications: "Who, me? But I never studied the classics!" I hate to inform all the daydreamers in Italy that the *Aeneid* is most often studied in middle school, which everyone has to attend, if for nothing else than to be on the right side of compulsory education laws. In middle school we study the poem in Italian, not Latin—Latin comes later, in the *cursus honorum*, if you are stubborn enough to stick with the classics. And in middle school it is taught neither poorly nor in passing.

The *Aeneid* is in fact a fundamental part of a subject taught in Italian schools that is more epic (hence more legendary) than the name it bears—i.e., mythology. Its concepts can be summed up, for the sake of brevity, with the following formula for oblivion, which can be applied to every branch of knowledge: "Stuff you do at school." Mind the verb: The epic is not studied but *done*, meaning physically built, actually produced. In the case of the *Aeneid*, what you do is lay the foundations for *damnatio memoriae* once you have gotten a barely passing grade on your in-class assignment.

Ever since discovering the grief that life (or Fate? I'll try to clear things up later on in this essay) dealt Virgil, I have done nothing but repeat, "He changed his mind in the end!" to those who scornfully dismiss the *Aeneid* as a product of propaganda for Augustus—a product, they incorrectly state, which pales in comparison to the models that inspired it, the *Iliad* and the *Odyssey*. Moreover, such occasions for defending Virgil rarely ever happen, because no one has ever taken the initiative to for whatever reason bring up the *Aeneid*—clearly I hang out with the wrong people. And whenever I have brought up the *Aeneid*, the snorts, sympathetic smiles, annoyed looks, and aforementioned excuses with which my mumbled words were met made me quickly change the subject—in any case, that must have happened a total of once or twice since middle school.

So now the time has come to do justice to the *Aeneid* and pay the poem its due. To do that, we all have to refresh our memories. Before writing this, I had to, too: I had practically forgotten having read the *Aeneid*.

* * *

There is this scene in Book 4 of the *Odyssey*. At the end of a feast at the palace in Sparta, Telemachus—having left Ithaca in search of his father—and Menelaus burst into tears, overwhelmed by recollections of the suffering at Troy. As if such were possible, their grief is made more acute by talking about it, so Helen pours a mysterious Egyptian drug, nepenthe, into the wine that her husband and his guests are drinking. The potion doesn't erase what they have suffered but eases their pain by keeping them from remembering any further.

Rereading the *Aeneid* a few months ago was just like tasting the poetry of Virgil without first lacing it with a painkiller. It wasn't the first time I was reading the poem, quite the contrary, but it was the first time I caught sight of the stabbing wound lurking underneath each line. I often wondered what had kept me from understanding the *Aeneid* before. What had prevented me from remembering it and identifying with it beside the need to know it inside out for an upcoming test? The search for an answer to my questions became an obsession once I realized, upon reopening Virgil's epic, that I remembered absolutely nothing about it save for a few images and the sequence of events.

In truth, rereading the *Aeneid* in the spring of 2020 disturbed me. I felt like I was holding an unpublished manuscript in my hands, a story that had never been told before that I was preparing to discover for the first time. I started telling people close to me what scared me the most about the historic setback that we were all experiencing, and I did so by way of the *Aeneid*. Unexpectedly, we understood one another, and if not better than before, certainly with greater honesty.

Virgil's verses were liberating. It was liberating to recognize that hurt begets hurt and is therefore an outrage, that fear cannot be shouted down, that hard work is a huge burden that we would happily forgo, that things won't always turn out well, that no one in their right mind aspires to be a hero unless by force, and that a tragedy has very little to teach us when not enjoyed at the theater. At last, after years of proving incomprehensible and vacuous, the *Aeneid* seemed necessary to me, entirely on account of the moment in which I reread it.

The pandemic deprived not only me but a whole era of nepenthe. Once the anesthetic—which all of us have been living under from the day we were born—wore off, suddenly circumstances forced us to grit our teeth and fight the pain. But no one could recall how, because no one had ever been cut so deep. So here he is, three thousand years later, Aeneas, once more "passing through." This time he isn't trudging over Troy's ruins but over our own.

* * *

Let's pause a second before we begin. If you remember anything about the *Aeneid* (something specific, I mean, factual, not the usual dull trivia that you find on quiz shows or in crosswords, like "Sad hero who flees Troy with his old man over his shoulder" or "Heartbroken queen who kills herself"), I'm begging you: Forget that for a while, at least for as long as you plan on dedicating to this book; and if it's bound to be brief, so be it.

If, on the other hand, you have forgotten everything—caesuras, figures of speech, allusions to Homer and subsequent echoes in Dante—even better. It will be simpler and more honest to let yourself be seduced, to tears, by one of the most tragic human and publishing events in the history of literature. No dictionaries or cribs are required. Instead, gird yourself with as much empathy as you can. Provided you have any. If you do not, then think back to when you had your *res*—your affairs, your business—and squeeze out a tear.

The story that the *Aeneid* tells—and the story that I would like to tell you in this book—is neither the story of Rome nor the story of Aeneas. It is the story of a man. Not an ancient but a contemporary man—one from the future, if the future were given to us to know. Provided that there is no substantial difference in feeling, that pain is not relative, that the sting of defeat in Troy as it burns is no different from the sting of defeat in the Forum of Caesar just after it has been erected, or in the tumultuous Florence of Dante's time, or when we go through an anonymous gate at the airport.

In short, the *Aeneid* is a story about a human being, with all the hard work that living and being human demands, a human being who, despite hardship, puts up a fight, perseveres, refuses to give in, and nearly always melts away in order to continue being the same man. How many cities, homes, vacations, loves, habits, friends, foes, political ideas, and philosophical systems can you shuttle between in just one life? How much energy can you expend on all that? How often, in one lifetime, can you recover from disappointment?

Is there a set number of slings and arrows we can take? A hundred? A thousand? Ten thousand? Is there a foul limit, a blow too many, a fall from which we're allowed to stay down? What does the final disappointment, should it ever arrive, look like? And what would be its consequences?

The *Aeneid* shows us how we can never escape all the wear and tear of living. How we need to stay the course. To the bitter end.

2
WEEPING: THE STORY OF VIRGIL AND THE *AENEID*

My mechanical dry peace
fits in the palm of my hand.
My earthly peace,
void of anger, unknown to angels,
fits inside the white
spine of a book,
the four corners of the page,
commas, capital letters.
In calm prospects
the intellect eludes
matters of hell.
—GIORGIO MANGANELLI, from *Poems*

Aeneas weeps. Meanwhile a defeated Troy goes up in flames.

Virgil wished the same fate for the *Aeneid* when what lay in ashes were the republican institutions of Rome.

Even here to glory goes reward,
to things their tears, and mortal matters touch the heart.
(*Aeneid*, 1.461-462)

If to all things there are tears, who knows how many the

Mantuan poet shed in eight or nine years of never looking up from his work. Work he never finished. For the *Aeneid* is, after all, nothing but an outline. A first try. A rough draft. Just an experiment. And a failed one at that. One Virgil was dead set on destroying to keep it from falling into the hands of his successors. From falling into our hands.

Weeping in Cisalpine Gaul

Mighty Verona owes as much to Catullus
as tiny Mantua owes her Virgil.
(MARTIAL, *Epigrams* 14.195)

At the risk of splitting hairs, the ancient village of Andes is, pace Martial, more indebted to Virgil than Mantua. Today the area is known (though not universally) as Pietole, a center of a district bearing the name Virgilio. It was there, in that backwater village, that the poet was born, on October 15, 70 BC.

If Virgil's literary life is marked by omens, twists of fate, and watershed moments in history, all of which he observed close-up—having lived through Rome's transition from republic to empire, first under Caesar and then Augustus, and, lest he miss out on any of the action, dying just before the birth of Jesus Christ—his personal life began, like the *Aeneid*, with tears.

Starting with the origin of the name of his hometown. Mantua appears to have been named after the prophet Manto, the daughter of Tiresias, the seer from Thebes. The

Greek term for the art of divination, *mantikē technē*, also gets its name from her. After fleeing Thebes and wandering far and wide, unsure whether to stop in sundrenched Turkey or the southern Po Valley, a place swarming, then as now, with mosquitos, Manto somehow chose to found Mantua, and filled a swampy lake with her tears. We don't need a fortune teller to tell us which star Virgil was born under.

According to some sources, Virgil's father was a potter. According to others, a farmer or beekeeper. What is beyond dispute is that he was the furthest thing from a committed intellectual in the mold of Cicero, who, at the very same time, in 63 BC, was ascending to the Roman consulship on account of his calls for reform and his oratory—which he expected would explain to his contemporaries and future generations how the world ought to work.

The fortunes of Virgil Sr. changed when he succeeded in marrying the daughter of his employer, Magia Polla, thereby obtaining the small chunk of land on which he had spent his life doing backbreaking labor. This was the rural landscape that Virgil would later sing about in the *Eclogues* and *Georgics*—and that would not shield the poet from feelings of nostalgia, grief, and finally disappointment. In short, more tears.

It is clear that once the family became landowning and to some extent middle class, it placed all its hopes in young Virgil, whose hands were straightaway torn from the soil and nailed firmly to a school desk. Books and lessons, first in Cremona and later in Milan, insulated the boy from the cries and alarms of Rome, where the First Triumvirate of

Caesar, Crassus, and Pompey (60 BC) was about to sink into the quicksand of civil war.

Having breezed through basic education, the brilliant twenty-year-old could not have picked a worse time to show up on the intellectual scene in the city which would give rise to an *imperium sine fine*, the endless empire that Jupiter promises Aeneas and his descendants. Yet the situation would soon deteriorate even further, proving that there is no such thing as rock bottom. And, I'd add, no limit to tears.

So, around 50 BC (or a little before), a young man from the outskirts of Mantua decamped for Rome and the beau monde of schools of rhetoric, brimming with hopes, dreams, and ideals—thus completely lacking the foresight to make sense of the political turmoil of the times.

* * *

An explanation of what oratory meant back then is in order. Forget the incorruptible Greek voices of Lysias and Demosthenes penetrating the dark, and the mind. During the late Roman Republic, rhetoric was everything. The political scene was so disjointed that there was not even time for something to happen—and if something did happen it was hardly over before someone had spun it into a story.

Everyone—or at least everyone who harbored political ambitions (i.e., everyone but slaves, and even they would soon harbor them)—was given their fifteen minutes of fame in the Forum, a chance to declaim what was just and what was unjust, at least in their opinion. The art of public speaking, of making persuasive and eloquent speeches, commonly known as *ars dicendi* in Rome, had strayed further and further from the honorable sobriety put forth by one of the most celebrated and exemplary orators of all time, Cato the Elder. On the contrary, rhetoric had turned into a show: The speeches had become spectacles and the orators gesticulated wildly, asserting everything and its opposite, in performances that drew hordes of people, as if rhetoric was a form of entertainment not unlike the circus to which it offered itself up as a radical chic alternative.

What mattered to the modest Marone family, and what matters for the purposes of our story, is that rhetoric was still the only means to climb the political ladder, as had been laid out by the *cursus honorum* since 280 BC, when, according to the history books, Appius Claudius Caecus gave the first speech in Rome. There is zero evidence of a consul having ever started his political career without first delivering at least one speech in the Forum with style and confidence.

For example, it was with two speeches nothing short of astonishing, given between 81 and 80 BC—the Pro Quinctio, with which he effectively defeated the leading orator of the day; and the Pro Roscio Amerino, in which he (again successfully, no surprise) defended a young man accused of murdering his father—that Cicero quickly freed himself from the minor—miniscule, really—*nobilitas* of Formia to which he belonged. (Unfortunately, his speeches did nothing to free him from the ungainly chickpea-shaped wart on his nose that earned him his nickname.) But the gap between Cicero's origins and Virgil's, in terms of lifestyle, environment, contacts—in short, their human and cultural milieu—was enormous.

So, it was very reasonable and completely understandable—worthy of praise, actually—for Virgil's parvenu parents to pour all their resources into the study of rhetoric in Rome in order to secure the best future for their son—just as there is nothing wrong with sending your most promising offspring to Oxford, Cambridge, Harvard or, in Italy, Bocconi University, to study business, management, marketing or information technology.

Still, it is one thing to be born, like Cicero, in Arpino, a suburb of Caput Mundi, a suburb not of the capital of just any state but of the world, "the greatest reward a general could earn," as Lucan says of Rome in his *Pharsalia*. It is another thing entirely to be born on the outskirts of Mantua, surrounded by simple shepherds and provincial farmhands, in the humid and muggy fields, on the periphery of a peripheral city that had been part of Rome for less than one hundred and fifty years. Divided by the river Po into two parts, the Cispadana and Transpadana, Cisalpine Gaul was not officially annexed by the SPQR until 190 BC, and Roman law would arrive there less than twenty years before the birth of Virgil, in 89 BC, at the kind concession of Gnaeus Pompeius Strabo (no relation to the more famous Greek geographer).

Hence there is little reason to scoff at and no reason to be cruel to Virgil if he had his first moment of weakness upon reaching Rome, the first of fewer than a handful in a hard life that would be one long test of endurance.

Hecklers, who never cease to pop up in the biographies of writers who left a mark on the great ledger of literature, and whose absence from said ledger is a sign they were forgettable authors of forgettable works, insinuate that, when it was finally his turn to open his mouth and deliver his first speech, Virgil did not speak. He didn't have it in him.

He panicked, became confused, began hyperventilating, and went weak at the knees. (Cicero said the same had happened to him, though he was clearly kidding.) Who knows, Virgil may have forgotten what he was going to say or simply lost heart. He shut his mouth, if he ever opened it, and stood silently facing the crowd. And here I ask the reader for a rare show of empathy. Not to absolve Virgil (who recovered from the debacle to pen not one but three immortal works) but to absolve ourselves for the moments when we, too, have clammed up; besides, those at school are the last we ought to be ashamed of.

We may not want to resort to trusting the spiteful and envious, though they are among the most eloquent sources of the patchy history of classic literature. We may not want to picture Virgil facing such a—public—defeat, either. Yet it remains clear that the young Mantuan was unhappy in Rome. Miserable, actually. Not only because of the unbearable living conditions in a city where chaos seems to be integral, a part of its genetic makeup, practically baked into the concrete on the day Romulus founded the city, on April 21, 753 BC. (We would be justified in thinking that Aeneas imported Rome's chaos directly from Troy.) All the sources agree that Rome was chaotic, noisy, dirty, putrid, and populated by shady characters. I'm referring to ancient accounts, not present-day abuse hurled at this or that mayor overheard at a bus stop as you wait for a bus that will never arrive.

These same sources agree that Virgil was a mild-mannered, kind, courteous young man with sound philosophical values and noble political ideals. No temperament could have been less suited to Rome at the height of the civil wars, which would soon conclude with Julius Caesar being named dictator for life.

Weeping in Rome

Anyone who isn't moved by the following lines from the *Eclogues* has never been moved in their life:

> I was a fool, Meliboeus, to think that Rome,
> was like this place to which we shepherds often
> lead the tender lambs of our flocks to market,
> to think I could compare great things to small:
> puppies to dogs, or kids to mother goats.
> But that city reared her head above all others
> like cypresses above the bending viburnums.
> (*Eclogues*, 1.19-25)

More touching still is what happened to Virgil later. From then on, his personal fortunes became inseparable from his literary fortunes. When Virgil gave up rhetoric, whether owing to his debut in the Forum or not, the first to abandon him were his parents. Bitterly disappointed that their dreams of rising in social status were dashed, they had no intention of further squandering their hard-earned money. They stopped funding Virgil's lifestyle in Rome, one that could hardly be called dolce, busy as they were trying to save their small plot of land from being appropriated by Caesar for the re-settlement of veterans.

Retiring his toga (if he ever wore one), Virgil did not fold under the economic pressure placed on him by his elderly parents. He had already made up his mind as to what he "wanted to do when he grew up" and the ultimate aim of his existence: literature. A choice that, then as now, seems to have made those who heard it weep hysterically. Not Virgil's *lacrimae rerum* but real prostration, the death blow dealt to those who are told that their child intends to devote their life to the classics. It mattered little that in those days Greek and Latin were not ancient languages, but very much alive and of their time.

Virgil may have been spared today's quips about so-called dead languages, though surely he had to have heard the typical laundry list of apocalyptic questions that rain down on anyone who opts to study the humanities: "What's the point? What did I do wrong? Classics, really, in this day and age? Wouldn't you rather get a real job? Yes, but what'll you do for work? You can't possibly want to teach, can you? The future is smart tech!"

Virgil wanted to be a poet, and that is what he did, confirming my own feeling, based on personal experience, that the most difficult part of classical studies is not studying the classics (studying chemistry or architecture is, I imagine, equally demanding) but having to endure all the questions that revolve around the classics. And the consequent derision, of course. Because it doesn't sting to get a bad grade on a translation assignment as much as it does to hear people say that even if your translation is perfect, it serves no purpose, because, in a modern, progressive, market-oriented school system, studying the classics is totally pointless. (This is how I arrived at the conclusion that the number one enemy of the classics are the superficial and hastily formed opinions of the classics.)

But that burning sensation shapes, supports, strengthens, and rewards you with an extraordinary strategic tool: the element of surprise. Upon completing your studies there is something heroic about astounding bystanders, proving yourself capable of achieving something good and important, and silencing the naysayers who had always been rooting from the bleachers for your defeat, your ruin, for you to be guaranteed unemployment and starve to death.

As a matter of fact, those who choose to pursue a path in the classics despite other people's (unsolicited) opinions—rarely meeting anyone along the way who supports, encourages, or even, as it should be, cheers on that choice—over time develop a determination and self-trust that can exponentially increase their chances of success, whatever they choose to do. Whether it be deciphering a Byzantine tablet, creating the next Facebook (Mark Zuckerberg was a great admirer of Homer), or teaching (the most noble and deserving profession there is, the one guaranteed investment). Or else writing books about, for example, the unforgettable snatches of country life in the lower Po Valley.

That is what Virgil did with the *Eclogues*. And he did it, for that matter, in spite of all the haters.

* * *

In 39 BC Virgil made his literary debut with the pastoral eclogues—from Greek *eklogē*, "selected poems." More importantly, the poems got him through the emotional turmoil of watching the collapse of the Roman Republic and the start of another civil war in the span of a few years. There were those who chose voluntary exile, like Cicero, who fled from blistering disgrace before being brutally decapitated. Others chose sword and shield. Still others, suicide.

Then there were those who, like Virgil, chose the dignity of poetry. Often—almost always—all that people remember of the *Eclogues* is the first verse of Eclogue 1, with which, in Italian schools, students begin their study of Virgil's poetry and the scansion of dactylic hexameter. Therefore, the following line remains indelible:

Tìtyre, tù patulaè recubàns sub tègmine fàgi

a line rigidly recited all in one go and all in one breath, so that you wind up suffocating from repeating it from memory and hiccupping through the accents.

No, Virgil did not fall prey to pangs of nostalgia for the rural straight talk of his native soil. Nor was he willing to indulge in apolitical literature, literature pursued for no other reason than formal pleasure—though he did not shy away from the scholarly endeavor of tackling the alexandrine lyric of Theocritus. The *Eclogues* were Virgil's means of interrogating himself in verse, now that he was a man, and examining the choices he had made up until that moment.

His conclusions? Failure and tears. Why did he get no relief from philosophy, which he had studied a great deal of? Nothing seemed to help. Not stoicism, from which he had adopted an almost religious sense of duty, nor epicureanism, which valued communion and solidarity. Looming before him was the hollow spectacle of traditional faith, which had lapsed into canonical formulas and mechanical rituals, and the coarse ruins of politics, reduced to war and illegal trafficking.

The "fool" isn't just the shepherd Tityrus who tells Meliboeus about his bitter decision to leave the country and move to Rome. It's Virgil. He is the misled puppy who trusted in an order to dictate the course of events. He is the lamb who believed that righteousness was the be all and end all, as it had been in country and provincial life. But it turned out that Rome knew no bounds, nor did its sense of self-importance—a city without equals that "reared her head above all others."

Julius Caesar died on the Ides of March. Virgil's faith died with him. Meanwhile people could see the "stars falling precipitously / and trailing behind them their shining wake in the dark" (*Georgics* 1.365-367).

Under these sinister omens, sometime between the end of 44 and the first few months of 43 BC, Virgil beat a retreat to Andes. There he discovered that in his absence his family's lands had been seized by Caesar's chosen heir and adopted son, Octavian.

Weeping with Friends

The next day was the happiest of our trip;
at Sinuessa we were joined by Plotius, Varius, and Virgil.
No more honest men have ever walked the face of Earth
and no one is more attached to them than I am.
How we hugged each other hello! What joy!
(HORACE, *Satires V*, 1.39-43)

Questions without answers wasn't all that poetry bestowed on Virgil. It also gave him honest friends to pose them to. Horace's *Satires V* leaves no room for doubt that by 50 BC, still a young man, Virgil had befriended persons of letters in Rome: Cornelius Gallus (his closest friend), Varius Rufus, Plotius Tucca, and Asinius Pollio. Pollio was a passionate supporter of Caesar in Cisalpine Gaul during the first civil war with whom Virgil tried to intercede to avoid having his lands seized.

The bond between the most brilliant poets of Rome at the dawn of a new era had nothing to do with boyish enthusiasm or desperation. Fifteen years after Virgil arrived from Mantua, in 37 BC, we find the friends marching along the Appian Way, bound for Brindisi, with the ambitious goal of talking Octavian into making peace with Mark Antony. The third member of the Second Triumvirate, Lepidus, was by then relegated to the margins, a bit player, which in truth he had been from the start.

It's unclear with which arguments the poets had thought they could convince the soon-to-be Augustus to bury the hatchet. But it's clear that Virgil's political foresight, which had proved subpar in the past, had not improved with time. And it didn't matter if they arrived in Brindisi late, after Antony had already landed in Taranto and hastily forged a pact with Octavian. (If you want to know how strong that pact was, just consider all the turmoil leading up to their final showdown in 31 BC at the Battle of Actium.)

What is beyond doubt is that there was no shortage of wine, revelry, or fiercely beautiful snatches of the Italian countryside on their journey. The trip also solidified a friendship that would be the one constant in Virgil's life, which lasted up until his death and, as we shall see, beyond his death. In his satire Horace mentions Sinuessa, what is today Mondragone, a town on the border of Campania and *Latium adiectum*, the extension of Latium, and confirms that Virgil had by then taken up residence in Naples. The city, with its gentle gulf breeze and lively literary circles, became Virgil's adopted home, his final refuge from the anxieties of his age.

In Naples the poet would write the *Georgics*, a didactic epic poem in hexameters inspired by the works of Hesiod. Of the four books in the *Georgics*, two are devoted to agriculture and two to husbandry. Yet a certain bleakness had crept into Virgil's verse. He had seen a lot, and suffered greatly, for "fast flies meanwhile the irreparable hour" (*Georgics*, 3.284).

In the poem, nature is no longer just an unspoiled and idealized source of beauty, as it was in the *Eclogues*, but requires tenacity, grit, sweat, and frequent lashes of the whip if one is to tame it. Or glean anything good from it. Life had required the same of Virgil.

* * *

Anyone who has tasted the salt of *lacrimae rerum* knows that however powerful hindsight is, there is no point in looking back and wondering how things could have gone 'if only.'

It's a fickle power. It neither adds to reality nor takes away from it, neither absolves nor condemns. If anything, it causes more tears.

All we can do is ask ourselves what actually happened next in Virgil's story, after 29 BC, when he had finished writing the *Georgics* and an influential friend suggested he present the poem to none other than Octavian. That friend was Maecenas, a nobleman of ancient Etruscan lineage whose name, to this day, is the eponym for patrons of artists and intellectuals of all stripes.

Frankly, Maecenas was more middleman than intellectual, a humanist in the very broadest sense. Nowadays we'd call him a lobbyist. In his *Compendium of Roman History*, Velleius Paterculus describes Maecenas as being "of sleepless vigilance in emergencies, far-seeing in his actions, but in his spare time more lustful and effeminate than a woman." His privileged position as Octavian's personal confidant and political advisor gave Maecenas every opportunity to wield his powerful office at a momentous time in Roman history, on the heels of the Battle of Actium, when power was all in the hands of one party. In the hands of one man.

We have to acknowledge that the meeting (today we'd call it an audition) that Maecenas arranged on Virgil's behalf was one of the most bizarre in history. It meant finding an opening in the agenda of the head of the greatest empire then known, in the schedule of the adopted son of Divus Julius, who by apotheosis had directly entered the Roman pantheon. It meant earning the protection and (financial) sponsorship of the dictator for life who would soon become the first emperor in Rome's history and, therefore, the man who buried the Roman Republic.

An aspiring poet ambushing a sovereign while he is bedridden with the flu and reading an entire epic poem out loud to him—a poem over 2,000 hexameters long—is unheard of. Yet that is exactly what happened.

Forced to stop in Atella on his return from a campaign in the East, on account of a brief illness, Octavian sat through the entire *Georgics*. (Whether he listened out of interest or boredom we don't know.) Virgil read the poem aloud himself, from beginning to end, though apparently Maecenas would take up reading whenever the poet needed to catch his breath. In the end, Octavian was smitten.

By the time the *princeps* had recovered and set out for Rome again, he had given Virgil a task: to sing of the past, present, and future glory of Rome, to author a work that was greater and more immortal than the *Iliad* and *Odyssey* combined.

Any sensible person would have refused, if only out of apprehension at being compared to Homer. But not Virgil; he accepted.

* * *

Two years later, on January 16, 27 BC, Octavian became Augustus (the title comes from the verb *augeo*, to augment), he who would "increase" the glory, wealth, health, peace, and power of Rome and its citizens.

The following year, in 26 BC, Gallus, the loyal friend to whom Virgil addressed Eclogue 10 and whose name appears by way of dedication at the end of the book, killed himself after political accusations that remain unknown to us. Nothing about Gallus has come down to us, not a whiff, not a whisper, nothing. The senate—or what little was left of it under Octavian—meted out a *damnatio memoriae*; Gallus was to be scrubbed from the public record. Even Virgil was forced to rewrite the parts of the *Georgics* he had dedicated to Gallus.

Meanwhile, to the raft of letters he received from Augustus pleading to read the new epic, Virgil responded that he had just begun, to be patient.

But Virgil had stopped wanting to write the *Aeneid* long before.

Weeping in the Fires

Mantua bore me, Calabria took me, Parthenope holds me now. I sang of pastures, farms, and leaders.
—Epitaph on the Tomb of Virgil, Parco Virgiliano in Piedi-grotta, Naples

What some call exaltation is really just the need to believe. Virgil desperately needed to hope in something. More importantly, in someone. To set down in verse the end of that troubled iron age into which he was born and in which he had thus far lived. To hail in verse the imminent birth of the *puer*, the child about whom he sings in eclogue 4, who would usher in the resplendent golden age. After so many tears, the season of *iustissima tellus*, the dawn of a world where, at last, justice reigned, was about to begin. From then on, law, order, and peace would forever govern people's lives, and people would share in solidarity the delicious fruits of Rome. Of all this, Octavian was the epicenter chosen by Fate.

True, in 29 BC, Virgil said yes to the *Aeneid*. It's equally true that inside himself he said no, almost immediately. But he was careful to keep that from Augustus. After all, how could you contradict a semi-deity, the son of the god Caesar, who among other things had recently created the office of emperor? Virgil's contemporary Livy, for example, waited to publish the books dealing with Augustus in his history of Rome till after the *princeps'* death in AD 14. And a century later Tacitus still thought it prudent to begin his *Annals* after that date.

Sometimes, historical silence helps draw a merciful decorum over things. Thus, posterity has been spared the rumors of the entire Roman intellectual class, who for at least a century must have grumbled, with venom in their eyes, "We knew this is how it would end." Just look at Ovid. In the *Tristia*, he turns to Augustus and calls Virgil's poem "your" *Aeneid*, as if Octavian had bought Virgil's work outright. But nobody "owned" Virgil, not even Virgil. After once again being disappointed by Fate, the poet had nothing to offer but resistance. And poetry.

Not only did Virgil leave the *Aeneid* unfinished and

therefore, to his mind, unpublishable. But the parts he did finish were badly cobbled together.

If there was an area in which Virgil could seriously compete with Homer, it was formal perfection. Some would even argue that Virgil would win that contest, though I don't intend to play the umpire here. Suffice it to say that, substance aside, in formal matters the two poets were batting in the same league. Yet what we have inherited is a patchwork *Aeneid*. An *Aeneid* missing one whole phrase in Book 3, line 340, which prevents our understanding of an entire sentence. An *Aeneid* parts of which Virgil took out—a whole twenty lines, verses 567-588 in Book 2, of which we can get a sense by piecing together commentaries from the time—and forgot to replace, as if it were a test and he had left sections of it blank because he didn't know the answer.

It's almost as if we should disregard the epic's inconsistencies, the foreshadowing of things that never occur or the events that do occur but are immediately dropped and left dangling. Even the routes that Fate indicates get tangled up now and then, become unclear, as if not even fortune knew where things were headed. Take line 7 of Book 3, which describes Aeneas and other Trojan refugees as *incerti quo fata ferant*, unsure where the fates were taking them. It would be hopeless, even naïve, to attribute to distraction what was deliberately left out; they were not mistakes and it was not distraction. How, for instance, can the various names ascribed to Aeneas' son, the person who would give birth to the eternal glory of Rome, be chalked up to a typo? That is no small detail; it is the meaning and ultimate purpose of the poem. In some places the son is called Iulus, after the gens Julia to which Octavian belonged (1.267), in others Silvio (6. 760). Elsewhere Aeneas dies before having witnessed his birth (6.764). But outside the world of poetry, Aeneas's descendant could only have had one not-so-obscure name: Augustus.

Can we really accuse the poet who gave up years—and his eyesight—laboring over the *Eclogues* and *Georgics*, with a dedication somewhere between scrupulousness and perversity, of carelessness, absent-mindedness and clumsiness? No, we can't.

In life, you're either like Penelope, destroying with the pretense of rebuilding, in the expectation of something. Or you stop at destruction because you no longer expect a thing. Like Virgil.

* * *

He was not going through a depressive episode. He wasn't in a bad mood or having a crummy day during a dark month of an inauspicious year. Least of all was he throwing a fit, for throughout his life he never allowed himself the luxury of getting angry. Whenever he fell, Virgil shed blood and tears and got back up again. That was all he knew how to do.

That Virgil had almost immediately stopped believing in Augustus is demonstrated not only by his dying wish that no one venture to publish the poem as it was (something that would promptly be ventured). It is demonstrated most of all by the reluctance—the tact—of Virgil, who largely omitted Octavian from the poem, when Octavian was supposed to have been the (paying) protagonist.

The *Aeneid* is made up of twelve books. But in all there

are only three mentions of the celebration of Augustus (we'll look at them in detail in the chapter on Virgil as an unwitting "minister of culture"). All are related to the first three months—or less—of the Principate. There isn't one nod to the eight or nine years of Roman history during which Virgil worked on the *Aeneid* before his death. It's as if for Octavian time had stopped with the victory at Actium in 31 BC. As if nothing had happened after.

But time didn't stop after Actium. A lot happened after. More importantly, Octavian wanted his *Aeneid*.

* * *

Before leaving Italy, Virgil arranged with Varius to burn up the *Aeneid* if something should befall him; but Varius had insisted that he would not do so. Wherefore, when his health was failing, Virgil demanded his scroll-cases earnestly, intending to burn them up himself; but since no one stepped forward, it was to no purpose, even though he gave precise stipulations in this matter. For the rest, he committed his writings to the aforementioned Varius and Tucca, on the condition that they publish nothing which he himself had not revised. Nonetheless, Varius published them, acting under the authority of Augustus. But they were revised only in a cursory fashion, so that if there were any unfinished lines, he left them unfinished.[1]
—AELIUS DONATUS, *Life of Virgil* (translated by David Scott Wilson-Okamura)

[1] Donatus, Aelius. *Life of Virgil.* Translated by David Scott Wilson-Okamura. 1996. Rev. 2005, 2008. http: www.virgil.org/vitae/a-donatus.htm.

*

There's no better excuse for a writer who wants to drop whatever they're working on than to boast about their travels, field research, explorations, hikes, climbs, and spiritual retreats to "get into the mind of their character." The fact that in most cases that character, the entire plot of a book, even the underlying idea, has yet to be written—actually, has yet to be conceived—matters little. We tend to open any door to writers and curtsy as they enter. We tend to forgive all manner of quirks in the name of art and look the other way when they act depraved. But that's called hypocrisy.

The truth is, around 21 BC, Virgil had the idea—the need—to check out of Italy and escape the pressing demands of Augustus, who was begging for the epic so that he could launch the most important propaganda campaign in history. The emperor was running out of patience.

Virgil replied, saying that he had to go to Greece in order to retrace Aeneas's steps and verify certain details in the epic. To sound convincing, he explained that he didn't want to be guilty of a lack of seriousness in his account of the exile's journey from Troy. (This coming from the same man who deliberately mixed up the name of Aeneas's son.)

It's unclear what tracks Virgil hoped to find in Athens, what footprints he wished to pursue, for Aeneas is a minor character in Homer, second to Hector among the Trojans, perhaps even disliked by Priam, leader of the Dardanians (allies of the Trojans), and given only brief mention in the *Iliad* to make room for the prophecy concerning his future.

But after three years in Greece and Asia Minor, it was a fatal illness that found Virgil, perhaps brought on by sunstroke.

Augustus came to his aid and arranged for Virgil, now at the end of his life, to return to Italy. Whether Augustus was more interested in the poet's wellbeing or the *Aeneid*'s we do not know. Virgil died shortly after landing in Brindisi on September 21, 19 BC. His remains were buried in his beloved Naples, where his epitaph—supposedly dictated by Virgil himself before dying—still resonates for its clarity and concision.

Yet the story of the *Aeneid* was by no means over. On the contrary.

It was just about to begin.

Sources—informants—point to Tucca and Varius. Apparently, they were the friends who betrayed Virgil's last requests, which he stated unequivocally before dying, as confirmed by the passage from Aelius Donatus quoted above. Whoever it was, the real culprit was Augustus, who did not hesitate to entrust the *Aeneid* to the printers.

A handful of missing lines wasn't going to stand in the way of eternal glory. His glory, obviously.

* * *

So it was. So it is. And maybe, for a little while longer, so it shall be. Virgil, to whom life had always handed defeat, emerged victorious for the first time. Without having to struggle or put up a fight. Since 19 BC, the *Aeneid* has been an enduring bestseller that has earned a place in every scholar's home, from Augustan Rome to the Renaissance to the present day. Ever since then, no curriculum has neglected to consider it a foundational text, alongside the *Iliad* and the *Odyssey*. As we shall see, his biggest fan, his die-hard supporter, was Dante Alighieri, who calls Virgil "that benevolent sage, who knew all things."

Where the lucidity of the poet on his deathbed failed, the lunacy of Caligula succeeded. The mad emperor would set fire to everything that belonged to Augustus, including the library where the manuscript of the *Aeneid* bearing Virgil's signature was displayed in plain view.

3
Not What to Do but How to Do It: The Role of Fate in the *Aeneid*

I wanted to see you.
I want the fantasy of your hair
to sound the call
of freedom in the hours that drag;
your earthly wrists
to wave the flags of revolt
and indict delay, cautious
despair, time.
I require a look of outrage
and beside the violence of your being
insist you laugh the way you do.
—Giorgio Manganelli, from *Appendix IIA, Poems*

We spend all our lives trying to figure out "what." Restless, we barely give a thought to "how." We naively believe that the course of our existence is determined by an endless array of choices given to us, choices about "what" to do with ourselves, with others, at school, in love, in politics, in the world, among the stars and beyond.

Every day, "when" and "where" and "who" and "why" multiply the opportunities available to us, till they seem infinite. Modern-day versions of Plato's Er, we hungrily roam the aisles of an illusory supermarket. For every type of product, there are at least three or four equally alluring brands, colors, packages, and aromas. Everything seems inexpensive, or certainly within our budget, and if something isn't, tomorrow will cover whatever we purchase on credit today. All we need to do is reach out a hand. And take from the shelf.

No one promised that supplies would never run out, but that's the implication. We'd be fools to ask; that's the tacit agreement that the system we were born into is founded on. But even if we can't see it, there is always a firm ceiling. What gets lost in all the frenzy is that the range of possibilities has, from the beginning of time, been governed by something outside us. Individuals have the freedom (and privilege) to give that something a name: religion, philosophy, nature, chaos.

Or, as Virgil called it, Fate.

Fate in the Aeneid

There are fewer than a handful of before-and-after events in one lifetime. Collectively, some rare generations have the good fortune of experiencing only two: birth and death. Others are called upon to endure wars or natural catastrophes. Or, like our generation, pandemics.

These events are epic in the classic sense, and entirely different from individual pain, which may be brutal but remains particularized, for only epic events force humanity to ask what's happening to us rather than to me. At the end of the day, such events are extremely rare, yet they are capable of upending the "what," which is to say the rules of the game. And they force us to hurry up and redefine "how" we act—so that we survive, first and foremost, while holding on to our dignity. Because the only thing we have abundant influence over is the meaning of our actions. Some of them will save us, others kill us, most are tedious, very few are brilliant, yet all are necessary.

Our aptitude for barreling ahead and seizing the moment stems, you might say, from pragmatic *romanitas*. With the proverb *homo faber fortunae suae* (every man is the maker of his own destiny) we shield ourselves from the consequences of existence. Yet this famous phrase, supposedly coined by Appius Claudius Caecus in his *Sententiae*, by no means ignores the "what" established by Fate. Nor is its protection omnipotent—is there such a thing?—so that anything is possible *ex nihilo* and *ex abrupto*.

Man is the maker of his fate—or what the Romans called fortune, a neutral force that stands as much for the winds of chance as for actual winds and has nothing to do with your garden variety successes, upshots, victories or conquests. But what often escapes us is how human fortunes depend entirely on *the way* in which we carry out our actions. The "maker" always operates within the parameters of Fate. Again, the question we must ask ourselves is how to confront fate without throwing up our arms or falling on the floor.

That is what is meant by *fatum* in the *Aeneid*. (Though the word almost always appears in its plural form, *fata,* it retains its singular sense.) We do not fret about what will happen to the refugee Aeneas as he goes from place to place after fleeing burning Troy: We know by the first verse that he will found Rome. What remains in play, and needs to be told, is *how* it will happen.

Readers hold their breath as they wait to see how Aeneas will be tossed about; that is how suspense is created—not, clearly, by the vain hope for a happy, obstacle-free ending. Most of all, readers are startled to discover how Aeneas will endure being tossed about—and, without a lot of huffing and puffing, how he will get back up. Not for heroism or glory. But because he has to.

Because Aeneas can't do anything else. Much less does he know how to do anything else.

To summarize Virgilian Fate in franker terms before moving on: We're all playing the same game. And at the opening whistle we already know there will be a winner and there will be a loser. Everyone plays by the same rules, and Fate is the referee. The point is to see how we play this game called life, *si qua fata sinant*—fates permitting, of course.

"What" in the Aeneid

> I sing of arms and the man whom fate had forced
> into exile from Troy, to be the first to reach
> Lavinium and the shores of Italy, and who,
> because of Juno's savage rage in the heavens,
> was battered by storms at sea, and tempests of war,
> until at last he brought his household gods
> to Latium and built the town from which arose
> the Alban Fathers and the high walls of Rome.
> (*Aeneid*, 1.1-7)

"*Cano.*" I sing. Meaning I, Virgil, sing. I am the one who will narrate the travails of Aeneas who, as Fate would have it, was exiled from Troy and sailed to Latium to found Rome. Homer's muse doesn't sing for me. From here on out the poet is no longer a mouthpiece spreading the word of the gods to the people.

In his proem to the *Aeneid*, Virgil immediately announces his presence. He confirms that he personally has survived. Considering the Homeric model, it's hardly a choice one would expect. Some sources claim that these are not, however, the first lines with which the poet intended to open the *Aeneid*. Supposedly Virgil felt the need to begin his epic with the first-person pronoun, *ego*, as if he didn't think the verb *cano* (I sing) was sufficient to stake out his poetic position.

In his *Life of Virgil*, Aelius Donatus (relying on an anecdote of the grammarian Nisus) claims that the original opening lines of the *Aeneid* were removed ahead of publication. Here they are:

I am the one who played on the slender pipe;
leaving the forests, I marked off the lands nearby,
that the fields might yield as much as possible
to the eager husbandman—a labor that pleased
the farmers—but now Mars is shuddering . . .[2]

[2] Donatus, Aelius. *Life of Virgil*. Translated by David Scott Wilson-Okamura. 1996. Rev. 2005, 2008. http:// www.virgil.org/ vitae/a-donatus.htm.

I'm not sure it's worth it here to go over every hypothesis that has been advanced down the centuries either accepting or refuting the authenticity of these lines on linguistic and formal grounds (in a nutshell: the Latinist Rosa Calzecchi Onesti has no qualms about accepting them, the historian Paul Veyne acknowledges them with reservations, and the classicist Guido Paduano rejects them).

It might be more interesting to play Virgilian detectives and attempt to solve the mystery based on the clues available to us. But that would be too easy. We won't be requiring the services of Sherlock Holmes today. Were the prosecutor (picture Cicero) to ask in his closing argument, "Who stood to be diminished, offended even, were the poem that tells the story of the birth of Rome to begin with the poet's own *ego*?" every reader would cry out, "Augustus!"

Suffice it to say that these four verses constitute a kind of bibliography: After writing the *Eclogues* (note the slender pipe) and the *Georgics* (the fields, the ongoing struggle between field and forest), Virgil is now proudly poised to sing the epic tale of Aeneas. Whatever the truth is, the phrase *arma virumque cano* (I sing of arms and the man) almost immediately became shorthand for the beginning of the *Aeneid*.

Which brings us to the "what." To the plot. A Trojan hero, *fato profugos*, whom fate had forced into exile, sails far and wide, bearing the brunt of Juno's wrath, until he lands on the shores of Latium. There, after a war with the locals, he founds a city with lofty walls and calls it Rome. Is this a new story, one never heard before, never even imagined?

Was Virgil's aim to bowl over readers? To shock, or worse, unsettle them? Looking for surprise or plot twists in the *Aeneid* is the worst way to read the poem and grasp its meaning—and the fastest way to end up disappointed. Besides, the very nature of the poem prevents Virgil from shocking us.

The plot of the *Aeneid* is not episodic—where every adventure introduces original scenarios that, once completed, lead to the next adventure. Instead, it's a tale with "a mission": the final founding of Rome. That mission is decided by Fate and revealed to the reader in the second line with no pretense of suspense whatsoever.

Think for a second about the proems to the *Iliad* and *Odyssey*. In the *Aeneid* we are not asked to find out what the terrible wrath of the protagonist will lead to nor to follow the nostos of a man of many resources on his journey home. A city must be founded. That is Aeneas' ultimate goal, it is decided by fate, and it is patently clear from the start. Does that mean that nothing happens in the *Aeneid*? That we must endure listening to a story we've already heard before?

In reality, a lot happens. The hero of the *Aeneid* is a servant of fate, a defeated man, a traveler, a lover, a captain, and finally the founder of a city—in that order. The action unfolds in Asia, North Africa, and Europe, on land and sea, in heaven and hell. Voyages, shipwrecks, battles, sieges, romances, apparitions, births, and deaths follow in quick succession. As do heroes, traitors, mothers, fathers, wives, lovers, teenagers, virgin warriors, and ghosts. There is even a queen who makes love in a grotto and later kills herself.

So much happens, though we ought to bear in mind that "what happens" is decided by Fate. That's the space within which Aeneas—and the reader—are free to move. And, as we shall see, it's plenty.

* * *

Everyone, since the time of Homer, knew the legend at the center of the *Aeneid*. And because nearly nothing is documented prior to Homer, we can hazard to say the legend has always been known.

To counter the curious astigmatism that sees all ancient authors as diligently writing about the same subjects at the same moment in history—even when two or three centuries separate one author from another ("Whatever, it's all the classics!")—it is worth remembering that eight hundred years separate the song of Homer's muse and the song that Virgil proudly laid claim to. A Roman reader at the end of the first century BC would have already heard the story of Aeneas many times over, in many different guises, on many different occasions. More importantly, Virgil was not relying on the gullibility of distracted readers so forgetful as to greet as new, or almost new, a saga rooted in the Greco-Roman epic. That would be a little like someone today expecting the Nobel Prize for authoring an original story about a man in the middle of the journey of his life who travels to the hereafter—and hoping no one remembers Dante Alighieri.

These buts and yets might be taken as givens, but I still care about them a lot. I feel a serious need to respond to all the mean comments from people who think Virgil copied Homer (and sadistically add, more often than not, "And he didn't even copy him that well!"). The time has come to expose the lies that prompt people to say Virgil was short on talent and imagination and had to resort to plagiarizing Homer.

"No, thanks, I'm not reading the *Aeneid*. I've already read the *Odyssey*," someone once told me, as if reading one exempted you from reading the other. As if reading Jonathan Franzen's *The Corrections* means you can skip Sandro Veronesi's *The Hummingbird*.

The time has come to get clarity and right a lot of wrongs. There's no need to probe the structuralism of Claude Lévi-Strauss and Ferdinand de Saussure, no point in fishing out the oft-repeated motto of people who want for invention—but have a knack for imitation—that says that every story is really a revisitation of other stories (some more, some less faithful), because, when you get down to it, we are all standing on the shoulders of giants (even if the giants are never mentioned in the bibliography). Anyone who still thinks that a story about a context (that of Rome) does not rely on the context that gave rise to the story itself, and that therefore it's possible to find an unspoiled intellectual wilderness, a Platonic realm full of fresh ideas, will be disappointed when all's said and done.

It isn't a question of cultural roots, ideological colonization or pre-/post-conditioning—all highly dangerous theories, as far as I can tell, often brandished by people with a propensity toward identity-ism and a disregard for reading works that challenge or celebrate. The point is, it would be like building the fourth floor of a house believing you can skip the second and third.

If every element of every story is related to other stories that it doesn't name but with which it coexists—and without which, in the eyes and ears of a reader, it wouldn't be a story but an incomprehensible, insane soliloquy—that is how Virgil chose to erect his narrative. There is no before and after in literature; everything is contemporaneous, because it surrounds the writer as they write, like air. And every debt incurred is transformed into credit when others come along to pen the next page.

Ultimately, the *Aeneid* exists because of Homer, not thanks to Homer. If Virgil recycles a legend first mentioned by the blind bard of Chios, it isn't to copy but to enlarge the legend, transforming a quick nod to Homer into an epic poem. And we are all free to do that, even today. For that matter, perusing a recent middle school curriculum, I discovered one assignment that asks students to write their own epic.

Readers then and now understand Aeneas's story precisely because they already know the *Iliad* and *Odyssey*. The opposite—a public forced to wonder, "Where's Troy?" "Who's Achilles?" "What war?" "This sure is full of surprises!"—would have made the entire narrative that Virgil erects pointless and vain.

An *Aeneid* without the *Iliad* would have been, to return to the previous metaphor, a fourth floor with nothing holding it up. I don't need to tell you that it would have brought down the whole building, which is to say, the ancient epic itself.

* * *

Okay then. Virgil's contemporaries were already familiar with the "what," the plot of the *Aeneid*, and no Roman was expecting a dramatic turn of events. So why should we today expect special effects? Why do we find Aeneas's voyage boring, uninteresting, sometimes predictable? And why can we not resist the urge to compare it to Homer's epics, adding sarcastically, "He did it better!"?

The reason we fail to understand the role of Fate—and venture to think of Aeneas as its puppet—we shall see shortly. The fact is that we have completely fallen out of the habit of standing still. The recent health crisis has taught us that all too well, and at too high a cost. On every occasion, we seek out the shocking. In a story—or a life—we concentrate on what is going on outside of ourselves, on characters and plot twists, without ministering to what is being produced inside us. Before something has even begun, we immediately wonder how it will end, demanding our dose of disquiet. And if things don't turn out the way we hoped they would, there are always prequels and sequels to suit every taste.

Change has become a virtue by default, and as a consequence we equate novelty with quality, an excellent excuse to update things for the sake of updating them. And if the result stinks, all we need to do is update things again and sail out into uncharted waters.

More importantly, we no longer understand the role of Fate because we have lost our faith in storytelling. We have stopped believing in wonder as an end in itself. In the power of fantasy that has no ulterior agenda. How ironic that today we trust all sorts of nonsense passed off as reality, but not the one *fabula* that an author openly declares a work of fiction, trusting in the unspoken contract of narrative by which a reader agrees to momentarily suspend their critical faculties and accept as true a story that they know to be, in large part, made up.

After all, the etymology of the word fate—a Latin term that bears no relation to the Greek word for fortune, *tyche*—comes from the past participle of the Latin verb *fāri*, to speak, which itself comes from the Indo-European root *bha-*, from which we get the Greek *phemi*, to tell a story. The origin of the lemma *fabula*, meaning story, is the same.

It's clear that Virgil didn't want us to take him literally. Just as nobody expected him to write an original myth, nobody expected a history book either. The Romans may have "sort of" believed in the legend that Rome was founded by Aeneas, in that vague way that people believe ancient legends about the birth of a city or a castle or a church without demanding archaeological proof. The historian Sallust said as much in *The War of Catiline*: "According to sources the city of Rome was founded by Trojan exiles who wandered about, under the leadership of Aeneas, at the mercy of fate." Still, a Roman would never have asked Virgil to account for the reality of his epic nor questioned its discrepancies with earlier versions of the story; for example, the episode with Dido is an original invention of the poet, who limits to three weeks what prior legends had extended to years.

An ancient reader expected neither novelty nor historical accuracy from Virgil.

They expected to be enthralled.

How in the Aeneid

Italiam non sponte sequor
I do not go to Italy of my own free will

This is one of the partial verses (4.361)—left unfinished by Virgil—that makes the "how" of the *Aeneid* indelible.

No, Aeneas doesn't spontaneously decide to hurry up and abandon Carthage, and with it a weeping Dido, to travel on to Italy. He does so to fulfill the will of Fate. Jupiter has already made the prophecy in Book 1: Founding Lavinium is what the future holds for Aeneas. Just as his son Ascanius must found Alba Longa, where, three hundred years later, Romulus and Remus will be born. The rest we know—we're living it.

Does that mean that, in the *Aeneid*, Aeneas is confined to executing, like a downhearted bureaucrat, Fate's plans? Must we admit that people who call the hero a puppet, a marionette, a shabby agent of forces greater than himself, have a point? After all's said and done, if destiny is already written, if everything is already decided, does Aeneas never make his own choices?

This raises thorny philosophical questions, which for centuries have kept us from fully comprehending the *Aeneid*. And for centuries have kept the *Aeneid* from reaching readers. Not because they are boring—that much should be clear at this point. But because of the depth of their consequences—and the depth of their pain, too.

That negated adverb, *non sponte*, captures the magnitude of the epic figure of Aeneas. A figure whose greatness is by no means apparent, at first sight, unlike that of an infuriated hero who desecrates the dead bodies of his enemies or one who blinds one-eyed giants. There is something far more subtle at play here, for the *Aeneid* is not a poem about power, as Simone Weil has it, nor is it about death. We are in the presence of something even more caustic—and more urgent, more necessary. Because no one holds on unless they have to.

Aeneas doesn't want to leave Carthage. In the first place, he never wanted to leave Troy. No one is a refugee on a whim; no one leaves behind their home unless their home is on fire. And yet Aeneas does leave. He doesn't even know how exactly he will get there; it is Fate that hoists the sails as he escapes his birthplace. And as he does, he weeps. *Multa gemens largoque umectat flumine voltum*: sighing often and wetting his face with tears (1.465).

Aeneas is anything but a quitter. He's not a victim of Fate. He doesn't execute the designs of a higher power complaisantly. Nor does he always trust fate; often he hesitates, becomes confused, makes mistakes, and later corrects course. Sometimes, he forgets about Fate—and finds, perhaps, a bit of happiness. Simply put, Aeneas endures.

He doesn't give up. When he falls, he picks himself up, dusts himself off, and wipes away the tears. Aeneas goes on, he is in no hurry to give in. He always follows through on Fate's commands. His form of despair is honest. It takes epic stamina to never quit. To not react to the latest setback as one too many. To not stay down after a kick to the ribs. To ask for nothing but for it to be over, that the next blow be the last. To never dare say "enough."

Not even to beg for a timeout. Does Aeneas expect a reward for founding Rome? Will glory be enough to heal his wounds and turn his tears into a smile?

No.

Aeneas knows all too well that there is no turning back from the path he's taken and that no one will carry him back to his home, now a graveyard, where he still would have preferred to have died instead of being flung elsewhere by Fate—"those others are three, four times blessed / for having had the fortune to die in front of their fathers / beneath the lofty walls of Troy" (1.94-96).

Once they have reached the destination that Fate has chosen, win or lose, there is no triumph. They are not lavishly compensated for their pains. They are awarded no consolation prize or merit badge. The one prize is being alive. Not yet swamped by the waves of existence. Not yet skinned alive by grief. It's not the events of the story that make the *Aeneid* unprecedented in the history of literature. It's *how* those events unfold and, most of all, how Aeneas reacts to them, that make the epic—finally, we can say it!—a masterpiece.

Unfortunately, we don't need to travel far back in time to realize that identifying freedom with omnipotence is tantamount to myopia and deadly folly; the tragic events of the last two years have reminded us all too well of that fact. Aeneas does not do Fate's bidding mechanically or despondently. The hero does not allow himself to be manipulated by anyone, for sometimes there is little choice—and other times there is no choice at all.

All one can do is accept things as they are. And after that set to work. Ultimately, the *Aeneid* presents us with an epic about consciously accepting that sacrifice is inevitable. Virgil's talent was to give voice to those in this life who do not do as they please but what they must.

To anyone tempted to reply that Aeneas could have resisted the will of Fate, or shrunk from it, we must respond: "Impossible!" For too long the word *fatum*, and all that it represents, has been improperly translated as "duty," a word whose value is relative, because it belongs to a specific era and a specific social context, and allows for the possibility of being changed—whether by science, technology, or, failing that, by prayer. The best translation of *fatum*—the most anodyne, the most lucid—is "obligation."

In conclusion, Fate can't be changed. It's neither friend nor foe. The *Aeneid* isn't a tournament or race. Bargaining is forbidden. Fate isn't even a war. It's simply the nature of being alive. Who will make it and who won't is determined by how soon they accept that fact.

* * *

Fas non est. It would be lazy to translate this warning as "it is not destined," when what it really means is "it is not given." It's not permitted.

In the *Aeneid*, Virgil does not shy away from dramatizing what happens when people rebel against Fate. Some may say "revolt" against Fate, but in reality refusing to comply with it is a futile exercise. It may indeed come as a surprise that the character in the epic who tries to resist his lot is Anchises:

> And so he spoke, and would not change his mind.
> We wept, my wife Creusa and my son Ascanius,
> and our whole house. We pleaded with him not to
> ruin everything, not to hurry out to meet his fate.
> (2.650-653)

It is Aeneas's elderly father who tries to shirk the demands of Fate. It is he who wearily blurts out that he has seen *satis una superque* (his fill and then some) during the Trojan war. Anchises wants to die in Troy. He's willing to take his own life and remain unburied so as to put an end to his suffering. So as not to have to abruptly pack up his household gods and slink off into exile. Is his act heroic?

No, his act is pointless.

Not because, a moment after, an omen—a flame that illuminates the head of little Ascanius—reminds Anchises that fate will not afford him the luxury of giving up. It's pointless because there's no more pitiful—or dangerous—spectacle than someone who thinks he can decide on his own when to quit in an emergency. As a rule, the spectacle doesn't last long—and as a rule it's a show of weakness. Aeneas then hoists Anchises onto his shoulders—the old man's infirmity is, according to some, Jupiter's doing, after the old man boasted of his relationship with Venus—and sets out for Italy holding Ascanius's hand.

The scene has become emblematic for all sorts of reasons except the right ones. If staying back "is not given" but carrying on is excruciating, one extreme option—maybe the only one, come to think of it—is to refuse to acknowledge it. Better yet, to repress it. But willful ignorance comes at an equally great, if not greater, cost. Fate requires that we place our trust in it even if we don't acknowledge it. Even if we don't understand it (and take no comfort in it).

Dido is *fati nesci*, ignorant of fate (1.299). No character in the *Aeneid* is described as more regal and commanding than the sovereign of Carthage. She first appears to Aeneas carrying a quiver over her shoulder, beautiful as a goddess, and while her court follows behind her, dancing in lines, she is "mindful of work and the future of the kingdom" (1.504).

Dido, in her single-mindedness, seems oblivious to everything. She doesn't know why the Trojan exiles have shown up at the gates of her kingdom, but she welcomes them anyway. (Line 630 in Book 1 is well-known: *non ignara mali miseris succurrere disco*, "No stranger to affliction, I have learned to aid the afflicted.") Worst of all, Dido can't grasp why Aeneas must leave her after months of romantic fulfillment. But she doesn't yield to Fate. Instead, she pleads with the man she loves to stay. She cries and cries.

Once again, she dredges up her resume of woes, as if there were a threshold of grief. As if, having suffered so much, she was now exempt from further suffering. In the end, Dido throws herself on Aeneas's sword. Her act is by no means a capitulation to Fate, let alone a triumph or declaration of independence. It's the dire consequence of her inability to give up. She chooses the certainty of death over the unknown and inevitable.

"We are not inexperienced in ills," says Aeneas (1.198). In general, everyone in the *Aeneid* suffers on account of Fate. Fate isn't an obstacle to progress but the engine thereof—and almost always leads to grief. We are well within our rights to ask whether the book we're holding is terribly sad. Demoralizing, many might say. But the *Aeneid* isn't a verse epic for depressives and downers. Much less is it a poem for damaged souls, fatalists, pessimists, and the morose. Besides, does all the bloodshed in Troy and Ithaca, do all of Homer's dead, make for a cheerful, optimistic ode?

We can't deny that the entire *Aeneid* is blanketed by melancholy, and there isn't one gesture of Aeneas, as there probably isn't one line in Virgil, that is not the fruit of an internal struggle. But that doesn't make it a sad poem, just a brutally honest one. Throughout history those who have loved the *Aeneid* most have been those who never stopped agonizing and at the same time never stopped interrogating what agonized them.

And writing about it. Like Dante. Like Baudelaire.

And the Gods?

Prayer won't change what the gods have decided.
(6.376)

One question can't help but emerge in light of all that has been said thus far. If everything hinges on Fate—whose reasons no one can know and whose course can't be changed—then what are the gods doing in the *Aeneid*? If not even the son of Venus—the goddess who will one day raise "brave Aeneas / to the stars" (1.259-260)—can do anything to stop impending Fate, how are we mere mortals supposed to?

Many gods make an appearance in the *Aeneid* and do what gods do: get mad, drink ambrosia, flaunt their beauty, herald the future, undergo spectacular metamorphoses, make love. But as far as concerns Fate, the gods are the same as mortals. Virgil's gods can't pull rank when it comes to *fas est* or *non est*. Nor are they there to provide an example of superior virtue or godly obedience to Fate. Like everyone else in the epic, the gods do what they can. And what they must. All the gods—with the occasional exception of Jupiter—are scared stiff by Fate. Sometimes they resist it, sometimes they resign themselves to it. They are almost always aware of Fate, so it is only within the space granted them that they rage and make peace.

In Book 2, line 54, we come across the words *fata deum*, what the gods decide, an expression that can be traced back to the much-debated "moira," or destiny, "of the gods" in Homer. Virgil's idea is totally consistent with the classical epic tradition: The world is an ongoing process with no beginning and no end, in which events are brought about by the clash of opposing forces. Fate itself is an emanation of what is to come to which mortals and immortals alike are bound.

But while in the *Iliad* and the *Odyssey*, Zeus exercises free will, in the *Aeneid*, Jupiter appears unable to act. His actions are conditioned by Fate, and sometimes appear to coincide with it: It's as if the gods' plans were incorporated into larger plans.

There is no hiding that this depiction of the gods has perplexed generations of Virgil scholars. The fact is the only thing that distinguishes gods from men in the *Aeneid* is the frosty privilege of immortality. Though, as in Homer, the warm and corruptible blood of mortals does not flow in their veins, the gods share in the human struggle that is life under the thumb of Fate.

It would take too long to enumerate all the critical inter-pretations of this phenomenon that have been put forward over the centuries. Most critics contend that the gods are merely a narrative device—the classic *deus ex machina*—for Virgil to keep his plot going. Others see their divine bitter-ness as a reflection of Virgil's own, human bitterness; it's hard to keep one's faith when everything is going to rot, now or in Augustus's day, and harder still when everything keeps getting worse. Yet some critics trace the reasons of this austere conception back to Epicureanism, the philoso-phy that most comforted Virgil (as a young man he studied the doctrine of Epicurus under Siro in Naples). Finally, there are those who claim it is a sign of Virgil's atheism, a highly unlikely hypothesis given the *Aeneid* was destined to be a cultural manifesto for the Roman Empire, implicitly connected to Augustus's plan to wrap himself in a veneer of religion.

Maybe it would be more appropriate to examine the

nature of Roman religion. It is spirituality, after all, so different from the West's Christian foundations, that separates us from the ancients. And precludes our understanding them.

For once we might try to change the perspective of our study and admit that it is not Virgil who feels spiritually troubled by Fate but us, his readers. Because regardless of all that happens, regardless of Fate, in the *Aeneid* no one stops praying to the gods.

* * *

There are many prayers in the *Aeneid*, all of them beautiful. During these moments of mysticism, Virgil directly echoes Alexandrian poetry, the restrained and delicate Apollonius of Rhodes being his favorite. Even if some critics have dismissed his invocations to the gods as "formal exercises" or "stylized passages," it's hard for readers not to be transported to higher and brighter realms as they set down the burdens of Fate for a minute. But there's no shortage of darker episodes, either, where Virgil seems to spy cruel, almost demonic forces at play in humans (9.184-186): "Is it the gods who put this ardor in our souls, Euryalus, / or is it our ardor makes a god of our desire?"

For sure, Aeneas prays to and honors the gods—always. The Trojans commemorate every arrival and departure with a sacrifice. These welcome and farewell ceremonies are part of the Greek tradition known as *epibateria* and *apobateria*, and previously described by Xenophon in *Anabasis*. Generally speaking, the hero's every act is carried out with scrupulous respect for customs, which will make him, as we shall see, the *pius* one par excellence.

Sometimes, readers can't help but smile bitterly at Aeneas's prayers, as when, in Book 1, his pleas to the gods to end the storm threatening to shipwreck his boat are met with an even bigger wave that comes crashing down on him. His petitions nearly always smack of desperation, for he already knows that they will not be granted: "For the defeated the only salvation is not to hope for salvation" (2.354).

So why does Aeneas, a creature at the mercy of Fate, which not even the gods can alter, continue to pray? Why does he waste his time sacrificing bulls and goats and erecting giant altars along his voyage when he already knows it will do him no good?

Aeneas honors the gods because that too—that especially—is part of surviving. Faith is the one tool that Fate has given humans, and humans need hope if they are to continue to live. It's hard for those of us educated in Christian dogma, which makes a distinction between what is true and what is false, to fully appreciate ancient religion, according to which everything is divine. And, therefore, true. Classical religion did not put into practice formal rituals comparable to Christian liturgy. "Doing" meant "believing." It was a pragmatic form of spirituality expressed not in the consciousness but in the actions of an individual. In the *Aeneid*, what is paramount is that Aeneas never stop "doing," that he demonstrate that, whatever happens, he has not stopped believing.

Were these rites merely a show of faith, an exhibition

for public consumption alone? No, Aeneas needs to demonstrate that he believes first and foremost in himself. That is the will of Fate. It demands that humankind hope even at the edge of the fire. And that, when all is burning, humankind hope harder.

Did the ancients really believe in such a heterodox religion? It's certainly not for us to sit in judgment of their spirituality. How could we? What do we know? We are not them. Aristotle said that the Greeks loved the gods the way every human loves their mother and father. Their faith did not need to be justified, let alone taught. The far more secular Paul Veyne notes, "Virgil may have believed [in the gods] the way a French patriot in 1914 could believe in 'France Eternal,'" which is to say, projecting the spirit of the times on to something or someone greater than themselves.

It's worth remembering that Greco-Roman mythology had no eschatological, etiological or philosophical pretensions. It was less concerned with religious values than with pure literature, written or (mostly) oral. Accounts of the love or wrath of the gods were, all in all, stories, in which the reader took pleasure, firstly, without being required to believe them or draw practical lessons from them—just like popular folktales in the agrarian tradition, entertaining horoscopes, bedtime stories told by babysitters or grandmothers, and all the stories that the sociologist Richard Hoggart classifies (nonjudgmentally) as belonging to the "culture of the poor," for the very reason that they are not sealed in encyclopedias. It's not by chance that every time Virgil tells a story in which the gods are called upon, he introduces it with the prudent *dicitur*, "it is said," or *fama est*, "word has it."

In conclusion, what counts most, what is most important—in the *Aeneid* and in life—is to circumscribe what one can reliably trust in. To give it a name, a place, a time. Then everybody can act according to their own beliefs. Some place their trust in heaven, others in Earth.

4
BEING AENEAS:
THE AUDACITY OF PIETAS

Who's to say the fickle soul
will not rest
one day, and, come to a halt,
reach backward
to trace its origins.
Any will do: a
fictitious genealogy,
a sacred family crest.
More troubling than the unknown future
is the absence of a past.
—GIORGIO MANGANELLI, from *Appendix IIA, Poems*

Heroes have an advantage in that their lives can be summed up by a single adjective—their "margins," as Elena Ferrante would have it, don't blur. Among the glorified, Aeneas is "the pious." And Italy his destination.

I am pious Aeneas, and my ships bear the household gods
that I rescued from the enemy. The heavens know my name.
I seek a homeland in Italy.
(1.378-380)

These three lines alone, spoken in Book 1, illuminate the

broader meaning of the *Aeneid*—and make the poem essential reading for those not planning on laying siege to a foreign city for ten years in the name of a woman and spending another ten years wandering home by sea. Not because you lack the time or strength to do so; no one would dare accuse you of that. But because your desire to do so wanes once you realize that such thoughtless acts are a testament not to courage but to supreme cowardice. If you have any energy left after the shock, it is here, now—while your house is on fire—that you ought to spend it. With all the discipline that requires.

Aeneas, says Virgil, is searching for a place to call his country, not for a throne to sit on or a kingdom to design a new flag for or intoxicating wealth to drown his sorrows. Aeneas travels in search of a place to stop. And, finally, build. Or rebuild, rather, for Aeneas is not a wrathful hero or adventurer. Aeneas is above all a postwar hero, a hero who has survived the bloodiest war of them all: the Trojan War.

He has no slaves or machinery or magic. All he has are his household gods, the guardian spirits of his scattered family, which he rescued from slaughter. And in his hands he holds the past with which he plans to build a future in Italy. And he has just one tactic to do it: pietas.

The Meaning of Pietas in Virgil

Anyone who has ever fallen down knows that cunning will not get you back on your feet. All cunning will do is make you slide further down. Guile, sleight of hand, and haggling may be permissible for the haves; for the have-nots, earnestness is what guides one through the slow process of rebuilding. You don't play around with what's broken.

Only those who belong to a lucky generation that has never known a crisis can mock Aeneas. Those who have never gone to bed at night knowing that yesterday's world will cease to exist tomorrow. Those for whom ruins are just a curiosity in a museum, because they have never been forced to remember what those bricks once propped up.

Too often Aeneas has been taken to task—made a laughingstock, even—for having arrived on the coasts of Latium despite being neither swift-footed nor resourceful. It's true, the hero doesn't possess any of the memorable gifts that would earn him a Homeric epithet—but who does? He is, however, skilled in the art of pietas. Sure, pietas might not help you slit your enemy's throat or silence sirens. But to recover from tragedy and found Italy, it'll do.

Translating the Latin word "pietas" is a challenge, which is why for centuries translators have refused to. "Pietas" is not the same as "piety," the devotion to a temperamental god, or "pity" for a human being who has been hurt. Textbooks often dance around its meaning with various paraphrases that border on mysticism. Or else they err on the side of brevity and call the hero simply "the pious," a word that makes him sound like a shrinking violet, doesn't live up to our idea of an epic hero, and fails to do him justice.

Latin dictionaries provide a straightforward definition of pietas as "a sense of duty." Aeneas does what he can throughout the poem (or almost; the time he is seduced by Dido is an exception). And he does it *de more*, as he should (5.95). Earnestly. His actions are modeled on *mos*, or mores, customs and conventions that are not the product of a religion but of the accumulation over time of knowledge, conduct, and traditions that turn a group of human beings (no matter how big) into a people.

The Romans used the expression *mos maiorum*, the way of the ancestors, i.e., those who came before us and worked on our behalf, to describe this patrimony of individual labors for the collective good—a people's knowhow and mindset, which gets passed down from generation to generation.

Therefore, Aeneas's "pietas" is not compassion or faith or mercy. It means having a purpose. Simply put, the hero works hard to do what he must, and do it well. Aeneas does what he *has* to as if it is what he *wants*. Erect, his head held high, his back nice and straight. That's not nothing—when faced with a catastrophe, it's everything.

Reading the *Aeneid*, the public must choose which side they're on. Are they with those who do or those who dawdle? More importantly, they must take stock of their own abilities. After a fall, we can't shed dead skin without feeling the sting.

Aeneas Prior to Aeneas

Tell me, Muse, by what offense against her power
the queen of heaven was so aggrieved that she

should make a man distinguished for his devotion
perform so many feats and face such dangers?
(1.8-11)

There's no such thing as ultimate victory. No triumph
is so great that we don't have the nagging suspicion that, at
the very moment we seem to be gaining the upper hand, we
are, in reality, losing. The good news that the *Aeneid* bears
is that, if things get done properly, not even defeat is final.

There was a time when Aeneas had yet to become
insignem pietate virum, the man distinguished for his pietas
described by Virgil. In all likelihood he was still a beardless
boy, yet to become a man.

Not even the name of the son of the Trojan shepherd
Anchises and the goddess Venus (their romance is told in
the Homeric hymn to Aphrodite) is all that clear. The two
hypotheses as to the meaning of Aeneas appear diametri-
cally opposed: The name either comes from the word *ainos*
(praise, tale, story) or *ainós* (dreadful, awful).

Raised and educated by mountain nymphs—or else,
according to other legends, by Achilles's mentor, the cen-
taur Chiron—Aeneas is referred to in the *Iliad* as the leader
of the Dardanians, an Illyrian tribe allied with the Trojans
that resided near the western coast of present-day Turkey.
In Homer, Aeneas never wins. But he never loses, either.

That he is out of place is immediately clear. You get the
sense that on the Trojan plain Aeneas is both there and not
there, that he is just passing through the present, waiting to
fulfill his future destiny. Like other heroes, Aeneas aspires
to gain epic fame (*kleos*) and be rescued from anonymity.

That will happen, of course, just not in that senseless war. Aeneas's destiny is to build with integrity and not, like Ulysses, destroy by deception. Fate wills him to be a good father and not, like Hector, take up arms and leave his child an orphan.

Aeneas appears in two scenes in the *Iliad*, though in neither scene does he play a leading role. He doesn't retreat from battle—even when his opponents are far from the weakest in the enemy camp. Instead, by divine will, the battle always retreats from him. In Book 5 of Homer's epic, Aeneas squares off with Diomedes, Tydeus's son, one of the fiercest Achaean warriors, who previously participated in the war of the Epigoni. Charging against the Trojans with flaming weapons, at Athena's suggestion, Diomedes kills Pandarus as he is fighting alongside Aeneas in a chariot.

Aeneas leaps from the chariot to retrieve his friend's body, so that it won't be left unburied. He strides over to him "confident as a lion / and [holds] his spear and round shield before him, / eager to slay any man he encounters, / and crying a terrible cry" (*Iliad*, 5.299-302). But baring his teeth at the enemy doesn't stop Diomedes from hurling a huge rock at Aeneas and nearly killing him.

What happens next is confirmation that, in the *Iliad*, disappearing is Aeneas's signature move. Aphrodite intervenes to rescue her son, covering him in a veil and carrying him off the field. Diomedes is so outraged that he even assails the goddess, injuring her hand. A ghost stays behind to do battle in Aeneas's place on the red earth of Troy while Aeneas himself recovers in the Temple of Apollo, where Artemis and Leto treat his wounds.

In Book 20 of the *Iliad* it is a mist sent by Poseidon that saves Aeneas from certain death, his challenger this time none other than Achilles. In this episode, retold in the *Aeneid* by Neptune, the reader first discovers that Aeneas's *pietas* proves stronger than his shield, which Achilles's spear easily tears through. The god of the sea gives just one reason for coming to the Trojan's aid (*Iliad*, 20.297-299): "Why should an innocent man suffer woes vainly / by reason of sorrows that are not his own when he has always given / suitable gifts to the gods that hold broad heaven?" In short, Aeneas has always demonstrated he knows how to do what he is supposed to do. Then why let him die, as he is not supposed to?

After all, Fate has decided that the end of Troy is just the beginning of Aeneas's story.

> This is not what his beautiful mother promised, not why
> she saved him twice from death at the hands of the Greeks.
> He is to govern Italy, land full of warfare
> and contending powers, and establish there a dynasty
> of Teucrians, and bring the world under the rule of law.
> (*Aeneid*, 4.227-231)

* * *

Even Aeneas's physical appearance is ghostlike. The hero is never clearly described in the *Aeneid* (or in any other passage in literature). There's not a gesture that makes him stand out, not a physical trait that could earn him a defining epithet. Sure, Virgil doesn't fail to mention the hero's extraordinary beauty—"Aeneas, fairest of them all" (4.141)—but his attractiveness remains fuzzy, with no detail that might distinguish him from generic *kalokagathia*, that classic ideal whereby "goodness" equals "beauty" and vice versa.

It couldn't be otherwise: Aeneas is not remembered for his body but for his more intangible aptitude for pietas. In the *Zibaldone*, Giacomo Leopardi notes, "So grave is the idea that Virgil gives us of his Hero that youth and beauty seem alien in him. It is as if we are hearing about them for the first time and we marvel (the marvels of poetry should not be like this), and we are almost unpersuaded, though they are entirely natural."

Readers of the *Aeneid* are never granted a glimpse of Aeneas's face. Perhaps when they try picturing him the hero's profile bears the modest dignity of neoclassicism corresponding to the ideal of "noble simplicity and quiet grandeur" proposed by Johann Joachim Winckelmann, who, incidentally, often used Virgil's poem to identify ancient sculptures rediscovered in Rome.

What comes across in every scene of the *Aeneid* is Aeneas's expression. His behavior, rather. The way in which his eyes are pierced by life—and how they react to it.

It's as if Aeneas were staring back at the reader. His gaze is always steady. Neither flummoxed nor helplessly blank. Aeneas regards the world with steadfastness—with an endurance that enables him to redress his wrongs.

In Book 4, Virgil employs an amazing metaphor to describe the hero's reaction to the pleas of Dido, just before the queen commits her fatal act, while he is preparing his fleet to leave Carthage:

> It's as when the northern winds in the Alps
> contend, buffeting now from this side, now from that,
> to fell an ancient oak; the tree groans, the leaves
> carpet the ground beneath the shaken trunk,
> but the oak is embedded in the mountain; as far
> as its crown extends to the high heavens, its roots
> reach down as far, to Tartarus; so he, though rocked
> on all sides by her words and shaken in his heart,
> remains unmoved, and the tears that fall are futile.
> (4.441-449)

Whoever accuses Virgil of giving Aeneas no personality clearly loves monsters and fools. Aeneas is anything but a heartless puppet who lets Fate dictate his next steps. On the contrary, he suffers a lot—and when he's hurt he's "rocked on all sides."

What makes Aeneas great is his resolve, his sturdiness. That is the skill pietas teaches: the ability to act like an oak in a storm. Even if the branches are buffeted by winds trying to fell the *ancient* tree, its roots keep it firmly anchored in the earth. Aeneas's roots are *embedded*: They drill down deep, through the center of the earth and on into the underworld.

Sturdiness as panacea, then? As cure-all? No, grief runs just as deep; there's nothing to be done about that. And tears are "futile" because they cannot change a thing. Resolve is more like a weapon. It prevents us from sliding downhill, from being driven from our homes, from joining the ranks of those who have been knocked about by life.

And, when the wind has died down, resolve shows us that there is no pain threshold—otherwise we would have died a long time ago. Instead, we are back at it, rolling up our sleeves, rebuilding what the storm has uprooted.

Aeneas After Aeneas

Ask anyone who has just finished rebuilding their home how many uplifting things they learned while swallowing their tears. Inquire about the "bright side" of human tragedy, about what moral lessons, intellectual propositions, and once-in-a-lifetime philosophies tragedy taught them. They'll tell you to get lost. Or if they're polite they might say, "I'd have gladly learned some other way, thanks!"

The *Aeneid* is not an instruction manual for how to construct grief and draw some lofty life lesson from it. Its twelve books are not twelve steps for finding out what catastrophe really means. That may be the most revolutionary gift that Virgil has given us: the freedom to finally admit that suffering is awful. That evil is chilling and that there is nothing heroic, or even very poetic, about enduring loss. That death is the ultimate outrage. And that, hitting bottom in a crisis, we are completely justified in wanting to put it behind us.

Aeneas is not in the *Aeneid* to fulfill some formative quest made with blood, sweat, and tears. He doesn't dream of telling us what he has learned from all his suffering—he restricts himself to showing us that he, at least, survived to live another day. Unfortunately, not everyone can do that. His father Anchises, for one, did not get to see Rome, having died on the journey. From the first book to the last, Aeneas does nothing but repeat that if it were up to him, he would have kept things as they were before.

Aeneas never yields to the temptation to give a moral or philosophical meaning to his plight as a survivor—not for a moment, not even mid-verse. He doesn't do it when the thick pall of grief clears for a moment and he takes a shot at being happy. There is no time like the aftermath of war for humans to understand what it means to laugh, because that is when we laugh at ourselves, we laugh because we're alive. Even when Aeneas falls in love with Dido—and let's be clear, he really does fall in love with her—we'll see so later on in this book—though he enjoys the moment, he can't help but think how meaningless all of the hardships of life have been.

For whole centuries the following lines have, understandably, seemed like the words of a coward. Then comes the terrible day when we are standing in Aeneas's shoes and these verses make us tear up, at least a little:

> If fate would let me live as I like and put
> my cares in order, I would live in the city of Troy
> among the dear surviving remnants of my people.
> Priam's house would still stand, and with my hands
> I would rebuild Pergamus for the vanquished.
> (4.340-344)

The conditional mood of his downfall is searing, the mood we form when we let ourselves wonder, "If I could, I would . . ." Aeneas has no doubts about what he would do if he could, if Fate let him. He would neither stay in Carthage with Dido nor leave for Latium. If he could, he would return to his city, Troy, to finally put his cares in order. He's even willing to rebuild the city with his own two hands to be beside his living companions—and his dead. It's only in a tragedy, when funeral ceremonies are denied, that the tombs of our loved ones appear "dear," for there is no greater violence than dying alone.

I don't mean to diminish Dido's heartache, which is equally searing. I've had my fair share, too. Just like everybody. And we all survived. Still, I believe those who accuse Virgil of lacking poetic verve, who claim the protagonist of the *Aeneid* dumps the woman begging him to stay with a line as cliché as "we're at different stages in our lives," are guilty of carelessness.

Guilty isn't the right word, and I would never presume to pass judgment. But people who criticize Aeneas for being a coward have enjoyed the privilege given to those who live in times of peace to judge the lives of others without thinking twice. Again, how one assesses the *Aeneid* depends entirely on the historical moment in which one reads it. In times of war, it takes on a different meaning: The prefix *ex-* no longer applies to a former lover but to a whole era that has been violently disrupted.

When Aeneas says that, were Fate to give him the option, he would choose his past in Troy over his present in Carthage, he is not disparaging his relationship with the queen. He isn't denigrating her or lying. Aeneas says something very simple to Dido. He is happy with her, very happy. But he would be even happier had his homeland—and life as he knew it—not fallen to pieces.

That's the only reason he has to leave again.

* * *

If you are still unpersuaded by the lesson of Aeneas, take a look at what happens to others in the *Aeneid*. By others I mean the future Romans' rivals, King Turnus and the Rutulians, whom the hero will combat after landing in Latium. And vanquish, obviously.

It's not that at the end the others lose—wars rarely have a different outcome—but how they conduct themselves in battle. Because if readers pine for Homeric heroism, they can find it in the *Aeneid* on the other side of the battlefield. On the enemy's side.

The original inhabitants of Latium, none too pleased with being invaded, act as if they thought they were in a poem written by Homer, not Virgil. They love imagining themselves in the *Iliad*; no one informed them that the *Aeneid* is another story. Their impulses take over, they enjoy their lives. They take pleasure in violence, as when Turnus attacks the Trojan camp, "tormented by chronic hunger, / his maw thirsty for the taste of blood" (9.63-64).

They love passionately and when they are offended proudly take up arms. Lavinia will not meet the same fate as Helen, so they say, and let Aeneas kidnap her and make her his bride. When all's said and done it's the enemies who do everything that a reader normally recognizes as befitting—as typifying—an epic hero: They tear their hair, claw their faces, wish death on their enemies, avenge themselves by beheading people, get drunk, and defend their city to the last. But this Homeric list of exploits quickly appears less like passion than enervating feverishness.

In the *Aeneid* the disorderly Rutulians either foam at the mouth, shout at the top of their lungs, charge into battle, or freak out. Prudence is not in their vocabulary. They attack their neighbor, shouting, *Audentes Fortuna iuvat*, fortune favors the bold (10.284). And they lose despite being stronger than their enemy.

How does Aeneas win if he's weaker? Thanks to the very thing we mentioned earlier: by transforming his fear into calculated bravery. By refusing to become irrational—which is the greatest risk for people under attack. On the battlefield—be it real or metaphorical—the goal of either side is to make it out alive. To limit the extent of the damage.

Whether you make it out alive or not depends on the kinds of choices you make when you've been brought to your knees. Whenever Turnus and his men are down, they panic and hurl blame and accusations at everyone. Even the gods aren't spared.

> Turnus shook his head. "Your cruel threats
> don't scare me, but the gods and my enemy Jove."
> (12.894-895)

Aeneas doesn't care who's to blame when he's been knocked down. He's already figuring out how to get back up. And that's how he has already won.

* * *

It's worth returning for a moment to interpretations that cast doubt on the status of the *Aeneid* as an epic poem. It's a novel in verse, they say, or, if you insist, a dramatic novel. Its protagonists seem too flat, cry too much, their fighting spirit appears sapped and half-hearted. Moreover, it's a story about the vanquished, about perpetual losers escaping the destruction of Troy. (True, Aeneas and his army do defeat the Rutulians, but they never conquer a kingdom; in fact, they have to build one anew and model it on the kingdom that they lost.)

Much has been said about Aeneas over the years—almost none of it positive. But worse has been said about Virgil and his *Aeneid*. Take the German philologist Eduard Norden, one among thousands, according to whom the *Aeneid* is a "dated" patriotic poem that portrays human nature as completely subjective, extremely disillusioned, and utterly pessimistic.

I will not tire of repeating: This book is not a defense of Virgil! I'm well aware that the *Aeneid* won't solve our problems. But at least it won't make them worse. I have come to realize that Aeneas displays none of the passionate feelings we expect in the poem *not* because he is incapable of feeling, but because he is kept from displaying them. He isn't cold or insensitive; he's powerless.

Whenever he suffers most acutely, Aeneas is forbidden to show it:

He puts on a face of hopefulness and suppresses his deep distress.
(1.209)

Right. In a crisis, we must muffle our distress. For Aeneas is not alone. Unlike Ulysses, who can cry all he wants on the shore of Ogygia as he longs for Ithaca, since Penelope and Telemachus are far away and cannot see his tear-streaked face. I'm not referring to his travel companions; Aeneas can't cry because clasping his hand is his son.

Therein lies the ultimate lesson of Aeneas's pietas. To carry on not because we want to but because we are not allowed to give up. To assume moral responsibility for the people around us. Bravely exercising pietas means not giving way to despair when we are unhappy, nor flaunting our happiness when things are looking up. Surrounded by ruins, we neither snivel indoors nor party outdoors.

Brilliant (and characteristically punk, albeit flag-waving) is Paul Veyne's response to those who accuse Aeneas of not showing enough remorse for abandoning Dido and criticize Virgil for wielding a pen with a hard heart. "Can you imagine De Gaulle dropping his duties for six months," he writes, "to lie in the arms of a pretty girl from London?"

If Aeneas does not shed the same river of tears as Homer's

heroes, that's not because he suffers less. It's because he suffers more. But he can't say that. And, as a consequence, Virgil can't write that.

One last note.

Aeneas never acts for his own benefit. The city he rebuilds in Italy is not a haven for him to retire to nor a banner to broadcast his fame. His voyage ends without reward and without glory, quietly taken up to heaven by his mother Venus. Despite his weariness, Aeneas forms a nation out of broken pieces, a nation he knows he himself will not dwell in. But which his son and grandsons will.

And after them, us.

5
WOMEN'S ISSUES:
DIDO AND LOVE IN THE *AENEID*

We have all our lives
to NOT live together.
The things we might have done
collect dust on God's shelves:
our touches are tainted
by cherubic flies;
our straw-stuffed feelings
perch like owls.
"Remaindered goods," cries the brass angel,
ten crates of lives, of might-have-beens.
And we'll also have a death to die:
a random, pointless, absent-minded
death, without you.
—GIORGIO MANGANELLI, from *Poems*

After centuries—millennia rather—of rigorous literary studies, when it comes to talking about women in classical myth people act as if we were all Madame Bovary. In the best of cases, I mean. In the worst of cases, the pages are populated with Cinderellas.

The psyches of male characters have been carefully dissected for clues to understand their mistakes and motives—in the case of Aeneas, mistakes especially. Philosophical theories, sociological models, anthropology studies, and all the usual responses to a society as chauvinist as ancient societies, have been built around the actions of Achilles, Hector, Ulysses, and others.

The fortunes of women, on the other hand, have largely been met with snivels. Sighs of "Poor thing!" greet the interminable list of ancient women who have been seduced and abandoned.

The Importance of Women's Issues in Classical Myth

The tragic fates of women in mythology almost never lead to an actual collective awakening and thus never to a concrete affirmation of female dignity. Nothing in poetry is mere fiction to be taken lightly, especially when it comes to myth, which, in verse, presents us with a specific way of seeing the world—and womanhood. More often, women's issues don't even cross readers' minds. Because we rarely look past the daytime talk show tears and attempt to understand why these women meet with misfortune.

We become indignant, and rightly so, at their husbands and lovers, their fathers and sons, who are always cowardly, greedy, shortsighted, insensitive, unfaithful, and spineless. And nearly always violent. When Aeneas visits the Underworld in Book 6, only women occupy the realm reserved for those who died of *durus amor*, hard love.

But our indignation soon gives way to disquiet and apprehension, to the bone-chilling question: "What if, in the end, the man I love leaves me?" So, we whip out a tissue for Dido, Nausicaa, Calypso, Medea, Andromache, Penelope, and all the other ladies, to dry their tears. And we just as quickly close the *Aeneid*, the *Iliad*, the *Odyssey*—the whole library!—and reach for the instruction manual on how to be the perfect wife, mother, sister, girlfriend, daughter, and ally.

"That's not my fate," we reassure ourselves. Meanwhile anxiety sets in. We don't dread being humiliated, hurt, quite possibly murdered, or losing everything: family, home, country. Forget our pride—even our names! What we worry about is being left by the man who claims to love us.

The result is that, while we're checking on the pie in the oven or looking for a top to go with our gown—euphemistic metaphors for our complex responses to the myth—men carry on undaunted, imposing their own ideas on us.

Look around. On bookstore shelves across the world, Homer isn't the only one saying how awesome and exciting it is to travel solo around the Mediterranean. On the contrary, the past few years has seen a spate of travel books inspired by the classics—be they actual travels or travels in spirit. Their authors? All men.

One faintly trendy way of avoiding the crucial question of women that the classics raise is to retell the story. Only the retelling remains identical to the original. Readers, so goes the thinking, might not relate to a woman being murdered two thousand years ago in Greece—here "ancient" becomes synonymous with "prehistoric." Let's set the story in the here and now, in our cities or in our tropical paradises, and have the women wear miniskirts and carry around smartphones. These retellings act as if readers are vapid and incapable of recognizing violence unless it's their own girlfriend with a gun to her head on their morning subway commute. More importantly they mistake for good faith, based on historical and geographic distance, what is patently done in bad faith, and continue to ignore the fact that women in the classics have a lot to say and even more to lay claim to besides pretty prose.

The same can be said of those halfhearted attempts at consolation known as "alternative versions" of myth. In these versions, Ulysses returns to Ithaca only to discover that Penelope grew tired of waiting and ran off with someone else. Or Helen tells Paris to stuff it and decides for herself which side she's on, spilling the beans about all the vile acts committed by Greeks and Trojans alike. Or, instead of falling on Aeneas's sword, Dido points it at his neck. These versions are not as alternative as they fancy themselves. Historically speaking, they're not alternative at all.

When it comes to furnishing myths with endings that depart from the original blood-and-tears finale, the ancients had us beat. It is hard to resist the temptation to make a sequel or spin-off of a successful story, and just as they're being hatched today at Netflix's California headquarters, they were hatched two thousand years ago in Athens. The Greeks didn't lack the imagination to come up with alternative endings to the most famous stories sung by epicists and tragedians. But these endings always leave a bitter aftertaste: the mouthfeel of too little, too late.

Moreover, they're like consolation prizes: There is always

something loathsomely disingenuous about them. "But later on" Medea gets to marry Achilles in the Underworld, said the ancients. "But later on" we find Helen, in Book 4 of the *Odyssey*, happily at home with Menelaus. "But later on," according to some versions, Penelope falls in love with Antinous, one of her suitors.

One feels like responding, "So what?" At least I do. Once again, I don't know whether to chalk it up to literary naïvete or deliberate dishonesty. No one is saying it isn't nice to discover that later on these mythological women found happiness. But anodyne happy endings can't heal real injuries. Nor do they relieve us of the responsibility to grapple with the texts.

In some contemporary versions of these stories, we watch men suffer the same things that they did to women, things hardwired in our imagination for two thousand years. It's the husbands who become the new victims of abuse, the disinherited, their throats slit by their wives. These versions even forbid the sweetener of consolation. Or, perhaps, of literature.

It's impossible to find relief in the application—even if it's only on the page—of Hammurabi's Code. Especially in books that mean to tell us that we must practice violence in order to effectively guard against violence, that women must do to men what for centuries men have done to them.

If there's no such thing as relative grief, there's certainly no such thing as relative malice. Murder is murder, whether it be on the plain of Troy or in the city of Paris. Whether the person committing it is a man or a woman changes nothing—adds nothing, takes away nothing. It's not as though if I do to you what you did to me, no one will ever do it again.

To those who say that provocations serve to awaken dormant consciences, don't hesitate to respond: Not at the price of betraying oneself they don't! And remember to add that, if some souls can't be stirred in the face of horrors, there's no need to put horror into practice. Those consciences aren't sleeping, they're dead. In some cases, they were never born.

In short, understanding the plight of women in classical myth is not a matter of turning the tables. Nor is it a matter of manipulating time and space to make them more relatable. Such experiments might have been enough to penetrate the shadows of the Middle Ages, when people lived their whole lives in the dark.

A modern society like the one we live in, which presents itself as the last link in the chain of technological and, more importantly, civil and moral progress, should finally have the courage to confront the subject of women in classical myth. More specifically: It should have the honesty to do so, to go a little further and dig a little deeper than merely being outraged over male behavior.

Because we're not talking about fairytales. No one is granted a happily ever after, except for the dead in the Elysian Fields—and that is for the gods to decide, not us writers. Nor are we talking about a writing exercise to give vent to our sadomasochistic penchants by making men suffer a punishment that resembles their sins; Dante's inferno has been fully booked for the last seven hundred years.

We're talking about classical myth. It may be the only field—certainly the least injurious, insofar as it is myth and not history or current events—in which we can try to grasp how a beautiful, educated (the female protagonists of epics are rarely illiterate peasants; they're almost always the daughters of kings who rule over cities and empires), independent, socially integrated, and strong woman could be driven by a man to utter (4.315):

(and I left nothing more for myself)

At least to ensure that Dido's grief doesn't remain a parenthetical aside, as it does in the text, where it has languished not for others nor for the courts of literary debate that have been in session ever since Virgil first described her tragic end, but for Dido herself. For her and for all women like her, to this day.

The *Aeneid* raises far more pressing and compelling questions about women than are found in conventional stories about a male hero who shatters the romantic dreams of a helpless princess. We've known for centuries that the hurt done to Dido merits condemnation. Now is the time to examine it more closely, to see what stuff that hurt is made of, and how it came to be. Not to perform yet another autopsy of Dido's grief, but to prevent other women's lives from "vanishing into the winds."

The Lesson of Dido

That was the cause of her death to come, the cause
of her hurt. She was not moved by honor or appearances.

No longer made a secret of her love. She covered
over her shame by calling their deed a marriage.
(4.169-172)

Ultimately, Aeneas has little to do with this harrowing
story. Next to nothing, in fact. We ought to make some
things clear right away in order to proceed apace. Aeneas
does "almost" nothing to Dido to deserve being crucified
by centuries of overly romantic readers. The word "almost"
takes into account the usual negligence that every man,
ancient or modern, can be accused of, allergic as men are to
certain subtleties of feeling. If Aeneas is guilty of thought-
lessness, then by association all men are.

Virgil's approach to the question of women is made even
clearer by his having chosen, from among the vast store of
mythical characters available to him, a hero who is not guilty,
or at least not guilty a priori (wherever the law doesn't apply,
opinions will vary depending on the individual). In concrete
terms: Unlike Theseus, Jason, Ulysses or Paris, Aeneas would
win any case brought against him. Handily.

Because no offense was committed. What crime could
he be accused of? Making a woman fall in love with him?
Inadmissible, says the judge, annoyed at us for wasting his time.

It's worth remembering that Aeneas is single when he
meets Dido. Specifically, he is a young father, a widower
with a six-year-old boy in tow. His wife isn't waiting for him
at home, weaving a shroud, trusting he'll be faithful. As we
shall see later on in this chapter, by the end of Book 2, his
first partner, Creusa, has already exited the stage.

Does Aeneas lavish Dido with promises? Does he

seduce her with tricks and cunning, bragging about how he'll buy her a castle, a diamond, and a pretty white dress? Absolutely not. He promises the queen nothing but his imminent departure.

Aeneas is anything but an arriviste with ulterior motives looking to gain, say, an empire or dynasty. From the start he makes clear to Dido his desire to found Rome on the coasts of Latium; that, as soon as he can, he will leave Carthage, the place that Dido is so eager to hand over as a token of her love. Most importantly, Aeneas never hides his unhappiness, not for a second, not at their most passionate or tender moment. His heart is in Troy, where the life he wanted to live went up in smoke. Moreover, no blood is shed during their affair, which is no small thing considering the brutality of human nature in classical myth.

There are no Minotaurs to vanquish, as on Crete. There are no usurpers to overthrow or brothers' limbs to scatter, as there are on the Argo. There are no suitors to execute, as on Ithaca. Not a single person is slain in Carthage, except the queen herself, and she by her own hand.

So why do readers shudder at Dido's heartrending cry? Why has the queen of Carthage become the emblem of all women who have been hurt or made unhappy by love? Because, though they may be reading the *Aeneid*, another story is playing in their minds. Many stories, actually—all of them terribly tragic.

Virgil's uncanny talent lies in his ability to bake Proust's madeleine into the most memorable episode in the *Aeneid*. If it's true, as scholars claim, that Aeneas's long stay in Carthage is Virgil's invention (magnifying what was originally a marginal episode in Aeneas's saga), the poet also manages to put the story in implicit dialogue with other love stories in ancient literature.

Thus, when a shipwrecked Aeneas washes up on Carthage, he takes the same steps as Ulysses on the beaches of Scheria. And it's with the Ithacan hero's eyes that Aeneas first glimpses Dido, and Dido is as amazed as Nausicaa by the new arrival. Their love story over, the ship that sails away is the same as the ship that leaves in its wake Ariadne, Medea, and Calypso in despair—making Aeneas not just Ulysses but Theseus and Jason too.

Having done nothing comparable to the actions of those other three gentlemen, however. Yet readers have long been beguiled by the sense of unjust tragedy that haunt the verses Virgil devotes to Aeneas and Dido. There was a tragedy, yes, but elsewhere, perpetrated by others, in other, remote stories sung by other poets.

Virgil reaches the climax of their tortured romance when describing Dido's despair. Verse after verse of Book 4 mirrors Homer's epics, Euripides' tragedies, Apollonius of Rhodes' *Argonautica*, even Catullus's wrenching carmina. These allusions, which readers at the time must have recognized by ear, make Dido's grief multiply, like an echo, and blur with the grief of every other woman in the classical world.

It's as if, in the *Aeneid*, Virgil has staged—without actually staging them—all the most violent actions of ancient heroes. And it's Dido who pays for them. When she suffers, she suffers for every woman ever violated.

Even if she herself isn't one of them.

* * *

Some readers may be wondering, "Well, if Aeneas is so innocent, then why does Dido kill herself?" But they need to realize that they are framing the question wrong.

For centuries, all readers have asked the same question of the *Aeneid*, except perhaps Dante, who didn't hesitate to place the queen of Carthage in hell alongside Paolo and Francesca. Surely such a question did not nag Virgil in the process of writing the epic. In Book 4, verse 172, he describes the tragic end of Dido in no uncertain terms, employing the word *culpa*.

It would be a betrayal to translate this word as "guilt," its primary meaning in Latin. A betrayal not of the *Aeneid* but of the law of human sympathy that forbids us from kicking people when they're down, even if it's just with words, no matter the cause of their suffering. I now prefer to translate *culpa* with its secondary meaning: "responsibility." To me this word opens up a space for more candid reflection. Moreover, it does greater justice to Dido's suffering without relegating her to the kid's table—a table she has been stuck at until now—by writing her off as a little girl who has been dumped by Prince Charming.

I take no pleasure in casting blame on Virgil's heroine for her own woes and forcing her to lie in a bed of her own making. (I hate to say it, but, in a way, that's exactly what Dante does.) Nor do I intend to forgive Aeneas for his awkwardness and shallowness, which sink to new depths in Book 6, when the hero meets Dido's shade in the hereafter and has the nerve to say, "I never thought / that my departure would cause you such pain" (6.463-464). For once we ought to recognize Dido's status as a woman with her own psychological dignity independent of her affairs with the men she loved.

How is it possible that for centuries her character has only been analyzed as a "jilted lover of _____" who chooses to kill herself "for _____"? Her grief is real, concrete, disconcertingly absolute. But by delegating responsibility to her we can begin to unpack her unspeakable grief, bit by bit, more closely examine what else it contains, and minimize the damage it does to other women.

Go find Rome, Aeneas! The question that I'm interested in answering right now is: Why is Dido so crushed as to choose death? More to the point: I would finally like to ask the queen of Carthage, and her alone—not her past, present, or future lovers—how are *you*?

Virgil does not shy from asking her and, in fact, does so openly. And he openly provides the answer in the *Aeneid*, which we fail to take note of, having for centuries been fed a romantic image of dames and ladies who are denied a life, on the page, and must wait for a prince to show up and give their existence meaning. But taking a closer look at the *Aeneid*, a reader realizes that Dido doesn't suffer for a lover who disappeared, but for a self-love that never materialized. It's not Aeneas who disrespects Dido. It's Dido who doesn't know how to care for and respect herself.

The risk of asking why it is that Aeneas leaves is that it gives rise to a suspicion. It makes us doubt whether we deserve to be loved. It legitimizes the idea that, when someone leaves us, slamming the door behind them (or pulling up anchor, in Aeneas's case), deep down we are to blame because we were not "enough." Not "good enough" or "sweet enough."

That is the emotional self-sabotage that overwhelms Dido before she takes her own life. Unfortunately, Virgil knows how to tell that story all too well.

* * *

For those looking for juicy gossip, I'm afraid the *Aeneid* is not a soap opera. Beyond a shadow of a doubt, Aeneas's love for Dido is sincere. There is no "someone else" in the story. There is, however, someplace else: not Carthage, but Rome, toward which Fate compels Aeneas.

There are no fleeting infatuations or games being played either. Aeneas's feelings for Dido have the heft of love. Of love when it is *magnus*, or great.

We have to admit that they made a nice couple. Perhaps we should start there, when Aeneas and Dido could claim to be happy together, and ask ourselves how it began instead of obsessing over how it ended. It's often in the first moments of a story that the end is inscribed. That's almost always the case—we can feel it, like a knot on the page as we run our fingers over it. It's noticeable, yet because we fear the truth, we prefer to ignore it and read on, engrossed in a plot that strikes us as surprising. "This time is different," we tell ourselves, ignoring the fact that, even if we strive to change the beginning, the end will still be the same.

If Dido agonizes over Aeneas's departure, that is because Dido was very familiar with agony before he showed up. Her grief was never resolved.

The man to whom my heart was first bound
took it with him and guards it in his grave.
(4.28-29)

In Book 1, line 630, Dido is introduced to the reader as a woman "not unfamiliar with woe." In fact, Dido never forgot her first husband, who was violently murdered, about whom she still speaks affectionately. By the time Aeneas arrives, she is a widow—and, by choice, a queen without a king.

Dido's husband Sichaeus was killed by her brother Pygmalion while both men, by the will of her father Belus, were ruling over Tyre, in Phoenicia. Jealous of his brother-in-law's popularity, Pygmalion has no qualms about ordering Sichaeus's death. Dido then sets sail for Carthage, bringing with her all the gold of her kingdom, in a memorable scene that Virgil mentions at the beginning of the *Aeneid*. During her years on the throne, though still young, beautiful, and courted, Dido roundly refuses all her suitors, including the illustrious African king Iarbus.

From the start, the weight of her unsettled past triggers in Dido an unhealthy obsession with betrayal. She accuses the dead Sichaeus of having betrayed her. "My first love," she says in Book 4, "betrayed me by dying." She forbids herself from ever loving again, lest she, in turn, betray Sichaeus. That's the sin for which an inflexible Dante will condemn her in Canto 5 of the *Inferno*: for having broken her promise to Sichaeus by loving Aeneas.

In the poem, only Dido's confidante and sister, Anna, seems to see through this swampy self-criticism. We all deserve to be loved. The dead do not cheat. If anything, it is we who cheat them. We betray their memory and make their death meaningless if we refuse to keep living because the pain is too acute.

In the *Aeneid*, it's Venus's fault that Dido "burns with passion" for Aeneas. But "madness ate the marrow of her bones," Virgil hastens to add, revealing that Dido is not impassioned, but deranged; not falling in love, but on the verge of a breakdown.

The exile and the queen meet in a cave. There, they are man and woman, nothing more. On an otherwise clear day, a violent downpour interrupts a kingdom-wide hunt. Everyone runs for shelter, and Aeneas and Dido find themselves face to face.

> Dido and the Trojan chief take shelter in the same cave.
> But primal Earth and matron of honor Juno
> give the sign; flashes of lightning are witnesses
> to their marriage, and nymphs ululate on the mountaintop.
> (4.165-168)

What is there to say about these verses? What can we add to the shrieks of the nymphs except to say that Virgil— either out of personal discretion or to avoid making the founder of Rome into a romantic caricature—turns out to be a master of "show, don't tell," rivaling Brontë and her splintered chestnut tree?

Aeneas and Dido spend the winter making love. They pay no mind to the gossip going around Carthage, fed by Rumor personified, or the criticisms of Aeneas's fellow Trojans forced to wait for their chief. You can imagine how much the couple worried about Fate, spending all winter long "forgetting their duties in the grip of disgraceful passion" (4.193-194).

And yet, at the height of their happiness, Dido's equilibrium, already unstable, begins to waver. There is no outward display of it, none of her actions could be called unsound, nor does she utter a word too many. Except to herself, a lot, and all of her words are in error. The queen grows confused and to justify her actions distorts reality. In her heart she knows that Aeneas is just a lover, that they made no promises, that theirs is a "furtive love." But Dido still prefers to tell herself that her man is her husband, that their clandestine nights constitute "a marriage."

Dido ceases to think clearly. She stops insisting on reality and instead covets the romance. She thinks she is Aeneas's wife. She looks at little Ascanius and imagines she is his mother. She loves to picture herself ruling over Carthage alongside her Trojan king. Thus, when the story that she alone has authored begins to unravel, an alienated Dido can do nothing but lash out.

To make things even more awful, no one around her seems to realize what is happening. Dido's pain comes as a surprise to everyone. In their eyes, she's possessed by Bacchus.

* * *

It would take Emma, the French activist and author of a feminist cartoon that became an international bestseller, to offer a convincing explanation about why the time has come to set down "the mental [and emotional] load" of our men. The men who stay and the men who go. Most of all when we analyze the *Aeneid*.

Despite what women have been told for thousands of years, we were not put on Earth to be cooks, cleaners, confidantes, tenders of the hearth, teachers of all children, ladies in public, and whores in our husbands' beds. We're not support systems for their emotional baggage. Our arms weren't made for raising a glass too many at the party, our shoulders weren't made to cry on. We're not the benefactors, editors, accountants, or unpaid sponsors of their projects, however mad or realistic those projects might be. And if we do simultaneously perform all of these roles for the people we love (without compensation, obviously), what happens to our own work? What, we mustn't forget to ask, is left in our own bank account? And, more generally, what part of us is spared in this unacknowledged squandering of the self?

Dido offers everything at her disposal to make Aeneas stay: her kingdom, her dynasty, her home, her name, her body. She even regrets not having borne him children in his image, the mortal version of Calypso's immortal offering to Ulysses. As a result, in the end, Dido has left nothing for herself. She blows it all on Aeneas.

She hits bottom, at least emotionally. Without his ever

having asked her to. Indeed, the hero may never even realize how much Dido has done for him. If pressed, he might
even submit that oldest of male excuses in his defense: "All
she had to do was ask!" The fact is Aeneas always wanted
to leave Carthage. And when he does, he sneaks away like
a thief, not saying a word to anyone, making sure that the
ships in the port are prepared in secret, without the queen
seeing, to avoid incurring her wrath.

I hope for your sake no one has ever looked at you the
way Aeneas looks at Dido while she's losing her mind. (It's
happened to me, alas.) He looks at her not with epic pietas
but with ordinary pity, the way you might look at a dog
dementedly barking at something only he can see and only
he is upset about.

"He stared ahead and firmly suppressed the anguish in
his heart. / After a time, he briefly replied" (4.331-332).
What follows is a scrap of a speech, in which Aeneas tells
Dido that if it were it up to him, he would have stayed in
Troy—and never have met her.

Yes, it's true, the critics have every right to say that
Virgil could have painted a more sensitive picture of his
hero in this scene. A little less blah, a little more sympathetic to Dido's plight than is suggested by his silence and
lowered gaze and mumbled words. Even if it were at odds
with his nature as a hero on a mission who is forbidden all
acts of tenderness save for planting his hands in the dirt
when he founds Rome, Aeneas could have said something
more supportive to the queen than: "Stop torturing us both
with your crying" (4.360).

But, to get back to the emotional "load" with which this

section began, we're not obligated to become the screen-writers of other people's reactions. No woman, least of all Dido, has to rewrite the lines spoken by men that we don't like. On the other hand, we are asked to acknowledge them for what they are, as they are written. And respond accordingly.

We also have to resist the urge to psychoanalyze someone who freely chooses "to get back on his fleet." Unless we are paid psychologists, we must not think that sophisticated psychoanalytic theories or disturbing childhood traumas can help us tolerate the intolerable. We don't need to go looking through the *Aeneid* for accidents in Aeneas's youth, for falls from horses or a turbulent adolescence—which may well have coincided with the Trojan War. We can't even hazard to dismiss him as a spineless coward, as people have long done, given his choice to turn his back on the most seductive woman in the name of a distant homeland which, at the time, is nothing more than a pile of stones.

Nothing in the *Aeneid* is so clearly stated as the reason Aeneas and Dido are denied a happy ending, given in Book 4, line 440:

Fata obstant.
Fate stands in the way.

But Dido can't understand that. She does not have the means of understanding it. She has not just been abandoned by Aeneas; as we have already said, she has abandoned herself. Dido is even deaf to the hero's one true declaration of love. Virgil writes that, yes, Aeneas is resolved to leave, but he is still *magnoque animum labefactus*: "shaken in his soul by his great love for her" (4.395).

* * *

The poet shows restraint and care when he describes Dido's motives for killing herself. The word "love" is missing. As is the word "man."

Then truly unhappy Dido, frightened by her fate,
prays for death; she is weary of the overarching sky.
(4.450-451)

Dido is hollowed out, tired of life. And because of this *taedium vitae*, this disgust with life itself, she chooses to die—such a motive was, moreover, acknowledged by Roman law. "Though I die unavenged," she says, "let me die" (4.659-660). To kill herself she takes up Aeneas's sword—after first cursing him.

How she takes her own life may be the reason the queen of Carthage appears to reject the role of a woman whose sole raison d'être is to be someone's wife: a role she faithfully played her whole life before she went mad. Dido chooses to die the way men in Rome often died: by piercing steel. Whereas women traditionally threw themselves off rooftops or hanged themselves (as the wife of Latinus does in Book 12), the queen mortally wounds herself with Aeneas's sword.

That is the end of Dido, who "did not die by fate, nor earn her death, / but died in misery before her time, plunged into despair" (4.696-697). Before perishing, she prays one last time to "whatever god is just and not oblivious to those whose love is unrequited."

We who are not oblivious pray for her and for women like her.

Romance in the Aeneid: Other Women, Other Men, and Virgil

Rarely do real-life romances reach the heights of passion found in novels. They are almost invariably quieter and more modest, though no less interesting. Somehow, they are also always tragic, even if their tragedies differ from the tragedies of epic poetry.

When it came to love, Virgil was no Aeneas: There's no trace of a Dido in his biography. We know surprisingly little about the private life of the poet, except that he treated his slaves with respect. On the other hand, there is all sorts of gossip about Catullus's lovers and Cicero's women (underneath the toga of respectability, Cicero was a rake). But there are other characters besides the protagonists who experience romance in the *Aeneid*. And perhaps it is through them, these other characters less memorable than the Trojan chief and Carthaginian queen, that we can learn about Virgil's deeds—and a bit about ourselves.

Every great romance has a before and an after—even if, in the thick of it, we have a hard time believing that. So it is in the *Aeneid*. Before Dido, Aeneas loved Creusa. After Dido, Aeneas loves Lavinia. We never have a clear idea about either woman, for they both haunt the poem, ethereal as ghosts; their specific weight isn't part of the main plot.

The first becomes an actual ghost at the end of Book 2. During the fall of Troy, Creusa, the daughter of Priam and Hecuba, is *fato erepta*, taken away by fate. What exactly happened remains unclear. No explanation is given as to how the woman, who a moment before was fleeing from the flames with her husband and son, suddenly departs this life.

If, as critics agree, the woman's abrupt exit allows Virgil to proceed with Aeneas's journey without turning the Trojan hero into a faithless husband (like Ulysses), we still can't ignore the fact that he fails to notice his wife has disappeared.

The following lines in Book 2 immortalize Aeneas as the most inattentive specimen of the male sex ever to have walked the earth:

> I did not know; I never saw her again.
> I did not realize I had lost her, and never
> thought of her until I reached the mound
> and Cere's ancient place.
> (2.740-743)

Shortly after, Creusa comes to Aeneas in a dream to urge him to leave Troy and found Rome. During their moving encounter, the hero tries to embrace her three times, and each time he fails, because she is an ethereal shadow, "like a light breeze, so like the wings of sleep" (2.794). Aeneas will repeat this hopeless if tender-hearted gesture when he sees the ghost of Anchises in Book 6, and it is later taken up by Dante, in Canto II of *Purgatory*, when the poet spies his friend Casella among the shades.

But in death Creusa betrays no regrets. She actually tries to cheer up her weeping husband. At this point, she says, Aeneas's grief over her loss is "insane." He must not delay. *Fas non est*: Creusa is not destined to be his companion in the "long exile" that will carry him to Rome. More importantly, Creusa already knows that Fate has not selected her to be queen of the new city in Latium.

After that, all memory of the woman disappears from the poem, "vanished into thin air." Aeneas will not mention her again in the *Aeneid*; only Ascanius will remember his mother, in Book 12.

I do not know whether love takes different forms and levels of intensity depending on whom one chooses to love. There is no doubt that the love that binds Aeneas to Creusa does not have the fire that will bind the hero to Dido. And yet it isn't completely devoid of sparks: Their love might not burn the house down, but, like candlelight, it's constant and steady. Aeneas's wife calls him her "beloved husband" and implores him to look after their son. More than anything, in the *Aeneid* it is Creusa who performs the supreme act of love by letting go of the person she says she loves more than life itself.

* * *

Lavinia, on the other hand, never says a word. Incredibly, Aeneas's future wife is given zero lines. But there are some things we can say about her.

Surely, the character of Lavinia is a testament to how much Virgil liked when the going got rough (poetically speaking). It appears that the Mantuan poet didn't care for easy triumphs, having arranged for his protagonist to travel far and wide only to choose a woman who openly loved someone else. Can you imagine Helen mailing back Paris's love letters?

True, Virgil needed a pretext for turning the last six books of the *Aeneid* into what critics refer to as the epic's *Iliad*-like section, i.e., a battlefield, especially considering that King Latinus doesn't think twice about handing over his domain to Aeneas. True, there is no better way to start a war than by placing women at the center of the action – true of the epic, that is; in real life, the real cause of war always involves money. But it is undeniably strange that, when Aeneas arrives in Latium, Lavinia has been involved with Turnus for a long time. They aren't merely flirting; they're officially engaged and expect to marry at any minute. And the girl doesn't just harbor warm feelings for the king of the Rutulians, but loves him passionately.

This dynamic alone is no reason to gossip about the author. However, there remains a well-founded suspicion that in this part of the *Aeneid* Virgil's usual flair for narrative invention was put to the test in the wake of his own misfortunes in matters of the heart. The connections between Helen's abduction and Lavinia's appear, upon closer inspection, tenuous. Aeneas doesn't rob anyone of a woman; King Latinus promptly offers up his daughter to seal the birth of Roman power with a marriage.

And when the reason for inciting war doesn't hold

up, Virgil complicates and confuses things even more. He involves dear Amata, the wife of Latinus, who is outraged about the fate of Turnus, her unseated son-in-law. Recycling the overbearing mother-in-law trope is one thing; starting a bloody conflict over this turn of events is quite another. The poet even concocts an old prophecy, according to which the past flight of some haruspices predicted that Lavinia would have a foreign husband. Enter Latinus, who promptly says that he had misunderstood the will of the gods when he promised his daughter to Turnus, to which Turnus offers his own prompt reply: Wait a second, *I'm* kind of a foreigner too. Ardea isn't Alba Longa, after all.

The one time in the *Aeneid* that Lavinia finds her voice, she communicates not with words but with a look. Here, the woman reacts to the sight of the man she loves (Aeneas is not far off):

Like Indian ivory stained with blood-red dyes,
or a cluster of lilies, white, that blush beside
crimson roses—those were the colors of her face.
(12.67-69)

Who knows how many times we have silently conveyed the same feeling as we gazed at the person we were not destined to be with, while our "official" partner was waiting for us, unwittingly, down the hall.

Who knows. Maybe, at least once in his life, the same happened to Virgil.

* * *

In the end, Virgil's emotional wounds emerge *between* the lines of the *Aeneid*. The personal and political anxieties of the poet lie below the surface of each verse. It has not escaped close readers, Paul Veyne *in primis*, how Virgil embeds the story of his own dispassion for Augustan Rome in the story of Aeneas and Dido's passion.

In Dido's inauspicious nuptial delirium we discern the blood spilled during Rome's civil wars, which divided people into two camps: those who supported Octavian and those who supported Antony (who, incidentally, was criticized for living with the African Queen Cleopatra out of wedlock). Furthermore, fifteen years before Virgil wrote his intense verses, the Roman historian Sallust declared Carthage "*aemula imperii Romani*," the one rival of Rome's dominion (*Catiline*, 10.1).

The best evidence of Virgil's loss of faith in Augustus lies in Dido's suicide—carried out, as we have said, in what the Romans considered the bloodiest way imaginable, by impulsively throwing herself on a sharp weapon. In fact—according to Ammianus Marcellinus in *Rerum Gestarum*—"*incubuit ferro*" is the same end that Cornelius Gallus chose when he could not bear the accusations made against him by the *princeps*. We will never know anything about Virgil's closest friend, doomed, like Creusa, to be a ghost, after all memory of him was erased by imperial decree.

Perhaps a trace of their friendship can be gleaned in the tragic deaths of Nisus and Euryalus, the young Trojan warriors, whose story is told in Book 9 of the *Aeneid*. The two perish together, attacked by Turnus's army after attempting a night raid. Each falls, as the Homeric simile would have it, like "a poppy beaten by the rain," his head "weighed down on a slack neck." One can sense Virgil's despair over the loss of dear Cornelius Gallus in the words Euryalus speaks as he mourns Nisus, guilty of nothing more than "having loved his unfortunate friend too much" (9.430).

A few verses on, the poet directly addresses the reader, asking that Nisus and Euryalus not be forgotten, going so far as to call them both "lucky" because at least they are still together, even if in death. Ultimately, on the rare—very rare—occasion when Virgil speaks about himself, he always sounds like someone who has met with tragedy and injustice. He too feels as though his love was betrayed, not by a man or a woman, but by an entire age. His resistance to his own day is halfhearted; you sense he is afflicted by the same weariness as Aeneas, forced to depart once more.

Virgil places his own regrets for what he has lost—his peace of mind, taken from him during the civil wars, and his birthplace—in the mouth of his hero. In the following verses (Book 4, lines 281-82 in the original, here translated by John Dryden), Aeneas mourns the loss of the happiness he felt in Carthage. But we can all too clearly hear the longing of the shepherd Meliboeus in the first eclogue (with its echoes of line 3) as well as the bitterness of a stunned Virgil:

Mute was his tongue, and upright stood his hair.
Revolving in his mind the stern command,
he longs to fly, and loathes the charming land.

6
THE GATES OF DREAMS:
THE *AENEID* DURING THE PRINCIPATE

I shield myself from you,
coming to terms with your presence:
with cordial, carefully chosen words
I tease you into not being.
Your face doesn't frighten me
if I know it amounts to nothing,
a random unfeminine
clot of myself.
This is the one way to shield myself from your blood;
for you always scare me
when out of nothing you approximate something.
—GIORGIO MANGANELLI, from *Poems*

Over the ages, all sorts of things have been said about
Virgil. According to the crustiest piece of gossip, he was a
troubadour for hire, a court jester tasked with publicizing
the exploits of Augustus to the beat of hexameters. This
widespread misconception suggests that the *Aeneid* was
part of a marketing campaign ahead of its time, each book
an ad endorsing the brand-new Roman empire. But a quick
fact-check reveals that, of the 9,896 verses in the *Aeneid*,
only 69 make explicit reference to Augustus.

More sophisticated theories, orbiting around Adam Parry's so-called Harvard School, identify "two voices" in the poem: a narrative voice, which sings the feats of Aeneas; and an allegorical voice, which celebrates those of the emperor. Other, less convincing theories claim the *Aeneid* is littered with agitprop and apologias so deeply embedded that not even proponents of theories that border on the occult can detect them, let alone the average reader. Then there are those who claim Virgil is a preacher or a carnival barker or even a prophet who alerted people to the coming of Jesus Christ.

This once, as we read the *Aeneid*, let's try to stick to the facts and not comb between the lines for what, in those lines, isn't written. Virgil was neither a minstrel nor a medium by profession. He didn't nurture political ambitions or delusions of grandeur which he sought to achieve through literature. In fact, the one time he tried to save his Mantuan land from being confiscated by the state, things didn't turn out too well. As he wrote the *Aeneid*, all he wanted was to be left in peace on the outer reaches of the empire, in Naples. There is no evidence of extortion or accounts to settle with Augustus, no erogenous tales about the poet and his close friend who would soon kill himself.

The record seems to show that Virgil had nothing to lose when he accepted to write the *Aeneid*. Because anything that he had to gain—fame, luxury, wealth, admiration, social prestige—had long been lost.

Poetry as Political Narrative

I already know how this is going to end. For what I am about to write, people will say about me what they say about Virgil: that I am on the payroll of some dark Augustan lobby or, worse yet, a crackpot monarchist. As if literature, and therefore politics, were a sports tournament in which recognizing the virtues (or shortcomings) of one side meant you were its most rabid fan. As if choosing a side—even just for a certain period of time, as Virgil did—were an act of servility and not the supreme exercise of free will. As if not choosing a side were even an option.

In the *Aeneid*, what I am most interested in investigating is Virgil's choice to accept the times in which he lived. I am not here to defend Virgil or rehabilitate his reputation—for the last two thousand years that has been the job of his poetry. Far less am I here to be sympathetic or give my personal opinions. I want to know what it entails to take a position when taking one is the last thing you want to do. What happens when you live through a moment in history that obliges you to pick a side—when "not picking a side" is still a choice, and usually a losing one. I am not talking about politics—not exclusively. What does it mean for a person to be called upon to rally behind one side or another of history?

Lives are at stake, and not because a dictator or sovereign suddenly orders, "Off with their heads!" But because human beings have always needed to believe in something or in someone. Even more so in times of crisis, when their only shield is a handful of convictions, and cleverly biding one's time never seemed so irritating.

Before writing the *Aeneid*, Virgil was free to choose. So he chose to believe in Augustus. Shortly thereafter, he was still free to change his mind. Whatever the case, understanding how Virgil, *qua* poet, came to make the choices he did is fundamental; as for his personal choices, his biography already says all we need to know. Why did he prefer that myth and not another? Why the dignity of Aeneas and not the ferocity of Homer's heroes? Why all the hard work of building and never the pleasure of tearing down?

It doesn't matter how Virgil and Augustus came to an agreement about the nature of their project, whether Augustus unsheathed his sword or gave him the nod. That's what novels are for. What matters is that, one fine day in the year 29 BC, Virgil sat down and began writing the epic poem that would finally provide the Roman Empire with an origin story. And just a few years later, Virgil sat down at the same desk and decided he no longer wanted to write that story.

Or at least he no longer wanted to write it *that* way.

* * *

The common misconception goes something like this: Homer's epics are freely sung, and Virgil's epic is the work of a sellout.

The time has come to specify what poetry means, or at least what poetry meant in Greco-Roman antiquity.

Personally, I still can't find major differences between then and now. In the classical world, making poetry was first and foremost a political act. Poets did not choose their words merely for the pleasure of their sounds but to convey the way in which the poet saw the world. Or imagined it. Most of all, a poet chose their words so that a reader could, in turn, imagine it in the same way.

The ancient poets were not shamans of primitive populations, pointing their finger in awe to give a name to a phenomenon that had never been seen or sung before. In the system in which they lived, the classical poets were primarily ventriloquists. Homer was by no means a beautiful, pure soul who was inspired to write the *Iliad* and *Odyssey* by the emanations of a muse on Mount Helicon. He was not confined to singing about his age; Homer created his age. By writing about it in verse.

I hate to disappoint those of you still holding on to the image of a bearded and bleary-eyed poet, innocent as a child, intently selecting from the stores of his imagination the actions of Achilles, Hector, and Ulysses—not to mention the gods. If Homer is portrayed as a naïf that is because his two immortal epics fail to name their patrons in the footnotes. We just have to read a bit more deeply to attribute the poetic gaze of the blind man of Chios to the dominant class of his day.

That does not mean that Homer was paid for his work or forced to write. God forbid. But it should be restated that no poem (or two poems, in the case of the *Iliad* and the *Odyssey*) would survive for three thousand years if it did not instill in its listeners a profound sense of belonging, if readers did not draw from the poem's geography, from its depiction of society—the way people made war or made love, their culinary traditions and funeral rites—a clear distinction between an "us" and a vague "them".

It isn't so much a question of roots or ancestry. The Spartans didn't believe they were all the offspring of Lycurgus, nor did the Athenians think they were all descended from Cecrops. It is a question of narrative. For poetry has always been a form of storytelling. Especially political storytelling.

Obviously, Virgil had all this firmly in mind while he was preparing to write the *Aeneid*. He knew that he was not being asked to stitch together a charming tale of romance and adventure. His mission was to create a completely new narrative for Augustus's Principate, which was itself a completely new thing emerging out of the rubble of Roman institutions. With one key difference with respect to Homer. Or two, actually.

First, Virgil was still living through the moment he was narrating, a moment that would forever mark the divide between a before and an after. And it is harder to distinguish between right and wrong when the train has yet to pull into the station and (usually unwelcome) surprises are the order of the day. Second, all the Romans would have recognized that the person who commissioned the work had a particular first and last name: Octavian Augustus. It was his own Principate whose origin story was being told, something Virgil, and all of Rome, had yet to fully understand, and yet to endure.

* * *

Virgil's genius was that he knew right away that the question to ask wasn't "Where to start?" but "Where to start *over*?" And to that question the poet had the courage to answer: "From the beginning—and earlier still!"

Who knows what today's political analysts would say. If the *Aeneid* were an election campaign, its claim (its slogan, technically speaking) would no doubt be "Make Rome Great Again!" The one difference between the campaign strategies of Virgil and Donald Trump is that Virgil conveyed his message in graceful hexameters, not vulgar tweets. More importantly, after the Battle of Actium in 31 BC, Virgil wanted to put an end to civil war, not incite another.

In all other respects, their narratives are identical. We might even accuse the American president of plagiarism were it possible to picture him as a sophisticated Latinist. Even the strategies implemented are the same. In the midst of historic political upheaval (arising from shaky democratic foundations, which were undoubtedly dictatorial in Augustus's case), they decide to pull the wool over the eyes of a bewildered citizenry by waving a flag of past greatness and prosperity.

It matters little that "again"—or, as the Latins would say, *etiamnunc*—remains totally abstract and vague, be it in Rome in 29 BC or in New York in 2016. Exactly when was the United States at its peak? Twenty years ago? Thirty? One hundred? And was Rome better off under Romulus, Scipio Africanus or Julius Caesar? It isn't for us to know, and nobody from on high will deign to tell us exactly.

It would have been useless to appeal to reason and respond that, at the time of its founding in 753 BC, Rome was just a pile of shacks along the Tiber, occupied by semi-barbarians, or that, in the third century BC, it wasn't very pleasant having Carthage for an enemy and Hannibal crossing the Alps on the back of an elephant. Logic is bested by nostalgia for the good old days, which in ancient Rome were better and older than normal and fiercely shielded from the dangers of luxury and frivolity, starting with Cato the Elder and the constant championing of *mos maiorum* (the custom of the ancestors). The actual living conditions of those ancestors, the Italic and Gallic peasants who lived through Rome's harsh annexation campaigns, didn't matter. There is every reason to imagine they had it hard, but there will always be someone willing to believe things used to be better.

Virgil's objective was to narrate what was to come *after* (the Principate) with the sounds and deeds of what had come *before* (Rome's origins). To endow the beginnings of the Roman Empire with the strength, intrepidness, and dignity of the beginnings of the Roman Kingdom and its seven kings. It was like watering down—to the point of expunging—all that happened in the interim, almost half a millennium of the Republic and its institutions. (As tradition, and Livy, have it, the Res Publica Populi Romani was founded in 509 BC with the overthrow of King Tarquinus Superbus.)

If you don't know how to communicate what you did, then you have not done a thing. So goes the principle of all effective storytelling. It's not as if the centuries-long

Roman Republic had a dearth of intellectuals and that, under Augustus, every previous literary work could be sponged away. But in the democratic era of consuls and senators, writers were too busy trying to change things for the better—some with philosophy, some with history, and others with speeches—to bother setting them in stone with a shared narrative.

If the Roman Republic was devoid of simple cultural manifestoes and full of complex treatises that no one but professional thinkers could access, the empire would take the opposite approach. To ensure that was the case, Virgil invented a genre: the national-popular, or folk, anthem. We have to acknowledge that it was the first of its kind, excluding the Homeric epic; however, it is harder to apply the concepts of peoples and nations to Homer's epics, since the idea of Greekness was as assorted as it was abstract.

In Augustus's Rome there was a nation—no longer an *urbe* but all of Italy—that had dire need of a new cultural identity to make sense of the changes that were happening. They needed to find a way to make the new narrative as exalted as possible, to make it neither cliched nor childish yet at the same time popular, so that everyone could understand, not just the wealthy and the cultured elite. In short, that everyone could say "we Romans" without having to consult the encyclopedia in order to figure out the story they were being told. They had been Romans before, yes, but now they were part of a different story, that of Augustus's Principate. What better way than to return to where it all began, to the fall of Troy? All of Rome knows the story of Aeneas, Virgil must have thought.

The time had come to tell that story again, as no one had told it before.

* * *

At the opposite end of the spectrum from those who see the poet as labor for hire, there are people who ascribe to Virgil, insofar as he is a national poet, the modern role of minister of culture. In this version, Augustus is an enlightened emperor, a Lorenzo the Magnificent, who doesn't stoop to the vulgarity of programmatic propaganda but entrusts his political vision to the elegance of rhyme. I disagree with this interpretation as much as I disagree with the former. In fact, I think that, once again, we must not misconstrue the business of power—now as then—nor overlook the role of the public, as we often do.

As far as concerns the idea of an enlightened *princeps*— enlightened or not, this is not the place to judge Augustus's conduct—it's worth pointing out that, ever since the time of Pericles, the governed have loved to surround themselves with illustrious artists and thinkers. That was true of Augustus's time, it was true of the Renaissance, and it still holds true today, at a time when world leaders don't miss a moment to take a photo-op with various celebrities. Come to think of it, it's also true for more modest echelons of society: In public we prefer to surround ourselves with the intelligent and dignified, not lie down with dogs, lest, of course, we end up with fleas.

It goes without saying that having dinner or attending the theater with someone does not automatically mean that you both subscribe to the same ideology, nor is it a public endorsement of this or that party. The same must have been true of the relationship between Virgil and Octavian. In fact, according to some critics, the young emperor was the one who benefited most from the association, at least initially; besides being his elder, Virgil was well-known and generally admired by Romans after the publication of the *Eclogues* and the *Georgics*.

As for the possibility that the *Aeneid* represents, in Augustus's view, the poetic training manual for model subjects, therefore placing Virgil in the role of Machiavellian strategist armed with hexameters, that would be nice. It would be touching to picture ancient Romans as highly sophisticated philologists, willing to toss out centuries of republican rule the minute they got their hands on a book that told the story of Aeneas. Unfortunately, it has always taken more—a whole lot more—than a beautiful poem to convince a nation to change political regime overnight. It usually takes a bloody civil war and/or an economic crisis.

As implied in the chapter on the figure of Aeneas, no Roman with a shred of common sense would have transformed their life after reading about the exploits of the Trojan exile who sailed to Latium. Because no one (or almost no one) believed in those exploits. No one expected the *Aeneid* to be a reliable history book. That from Aeneas was descended Iulus, and from Iulus, three hundred years later, Romulus and Remus, did not change a thing. Besides, Julius Caesar had just been deified in 44 BC at a crowning ceremony without demanding Roman citizens make it religious or scientific dogma. The new empire needed no archaeological or mythological or biographical bedrock whatsoever. Augustus was not seeking to justify himself; he didn't need to.

What he sought was collective adherence to his plan, and for that plan to turn into an ideology. It's conceivable that Virgil was not the only one operating toward that end, that all the intellectuals who chose to believe in Augustus's political project strove to do what they could. Or rather, did what they knew how. Architects erected forums and arches, sculptors chiseled statues and tympana and metopes, historians wrote histories, actors acted, gladiators died valiantly. Each of them was inspired by the patriotic idea of Pax Romana, the long period of peace and prosperity that Augustus promised by halting all campaigns of conquest.

About the relationship between the *princeps* and Virgil, Luca Canali writes, "Virgil poetically interpreted Augustus's edicts, and Augustus likewise used Virgil's poetic phrases to burnish his political testament." Does that basic relationship, in which the political narrative shapes reality and reality in turn chases after a political narrative, remind you of anything?

For too long our interpretations of Virgil have alternated between thinking he was a literary sycophant and thinking he was a literary stunt, because we fail to comprehend the function of a poet in antiquity. It was not his job to set down in rhyme Hallmark-style heavy breathing. Instead he was tasked with finding the right words to articulate—to influence—the times. Given his political relevance and bearing, we could conclude that the classical poet did what a social media manager does today. Many people might be horrified by my saying so, and they wouldn't be wrong. But it is nice to know that there was a time in which political dialogue was not entrusted to shouts or slide shows, but to an epic poem in twelve books.

And that—even more incredibly—everyone got it.

Black Mirror

> Aeneas admired and wondered at these scenes
> on the shield which Vulcan made, a gift from his mother.
> Though he did not know what it was he saw, he carried on
> his shoulders the fame and fate of his descendants.
> (8.729-732)

We have just seen how the *Aeneid* is not the Augusteid. And yet the emperor isn't left out of Virgil's poem. On the contrary.

Virgil's poetic talent was extraordinary, since he never gave in to the temptation to take the easy route by placing fictional characters in the ruins of Troy and having them ape the actions of actual people that a reader would easily recognize. In a move that Dante will adopt wholesale in the *Commedia*, the poet is unafraid and unembarrassed to call a thing by its real name and a person by their full. In the *Aeneid* it is the setting that remains fictional, while the references to current events and real people are very specific.

To make sense of the connection between epic myth and Roman history in the poem, we must pay special attention to, on the one hand, the timeframe Aeneas and his companions inhabit, and, on the other, the timeframe of Virgil and his public. Because what makes the *Aeneid* such an eerie masterpiece is the suppression of any sense of the present giving rise to a poem that is all in the future perfect—an epic poem in which every prediction was coming true at the exact moment in which the reader of the age would have been reading it.

To dig into the details, calculator in hand: Aeneas sets sail for Latium at least three hundred years before the birth of Romulus and Remus. Seven hundred years separate the wolf-suckled twins from the ascendancy of Augustus. Thus Virgil has in his hands both a myth of very limited duration and a history of almost a thousand years to condense—with the aim, however, of providing a narrative that only applies to the last decade. The *Aeneid* turns out to be, in large part, not the chronicle of a mythic past but of Rome's historic future—which just happened to be the present in which the public was living and going about their business at the time the poet was writing.

We can clearly discern the real cause-and-effect relationships between every act of Aeneas and the other fictional characters, and the situation in Rome immediately following the Battle of Actium. Readers of the *Aeneid* would have experienced a constant sense of imminent catastrophe, feeling somehow complicit in or witnesses to the story—or at least drawn into the action. The prophecies in the *Aeneid* sound so distressing because the Roman public knows perfectly well that they will come true. In fact, they are already coming true at the time the poem sees the light of day.

It's a bit like Charlie Broker's dystopian series *Black*

Mirror, set in the future but inspired by our current moment to ponder the implications of new technologies. Viewers know that nothing is happening *hic et nunc*, but one episode is enough to make them feel less comfortable about carrying their smartphones around. Exactly the way we are all always evaluating how we might react to a crisis. Had someone told us before, we never would have believed them. In the heat of the moment, we can hardly bring anything into focus. But afterward, when we tell the story, what seems impossible is that there was ever a time when such things seemed impossible.

* * *

The references to Augustus are concentrated in three passages in the *Aeneid*, and they foretell a future that by Virgil's time had already transpired.

The first reference is contained in a speech by Jupiter, in Book 1, aimed at assuaging Venus's concerns over the fate of Aeneas. "Be not afraid, Cytherea," he tells her, "the fortunes of your children still stand" (1.257-258). At the outset of the epic, Virgil describes in detail the history of Rome, which in the poem has yet to happen but for the reader happened a long time ago. Jupiter says that once Aeneas arrives in Latium, he "will crush its proud peoples," and that Ascanius will be rechristened Iulus by the gens Julia to which Caesar and, by adoption, Octavian belonged, and move the kingdom to Alba Longa once he turns thirty. The city will have dominion for "three hundred years" until a royal priestess gives birth to two twins.

Romulus will be the one to erect the walls of Mars and call his people Romans.

This is the beginning of the *imperium sine fine*—an empire not even Jupiter himself will place a limit on.

> And Caesar will be born, of good Trojan stock.
> His empire will stretch to the ocean, his fame to the stars.
> He'll take the name Julius, after noble Iulus.
> And you will welcome him in heaven when he bears
> the spoils of the Orient, and he'll be prayed to as a god.
> (1.286-290)

It has long been debated whether by Caesar Virgil is referring to Julius Caesar or to Octavian. But the mention, a little later on, of the closing of the doors of the Temple of Janus, which symbolized the preservation of peace and the end of "impious Fury," makes it all but certain that, here as elsewhere, the fated one is Augustus. After the Battle of Actium, in 29 BC, the gates of the Temple of Janus Quirinus—the two-faced Roman god of beginnings and guardian of thresholds—were ordered closed in honor of Octavian's victory. It is thanks to him that "the violent age will give way to peace" (1.291).

The symbolic act of closing or opening the gates of war must have made a great impression on Virgil; in Book 6 he even traces the Roman ritual back to an ancient custom of the Alban people. The gates of Janus would be closed twice more under the *princeps*: in 25 BC and again in AD 2, long after the poet had died.

* * *

In Book 8, Augustus and his victory in Actium are described in soaring, triumphant terms, and take on divine proportions. The shield forged for Aeneas by Vulcan depicts Roman history, from its foundation to the defeat of Antony and Cleopatra.

> The God of fire, who knew the prophecies,
> had carved the story of Italia and Roman triumphs,
> and all the children of Ascanius,
> and then he chronicled the wars they'd win.
> (8.626-629)

The ekphrasis (from the Greek word meaning "descriptive speech") clearly alludes to Homer's description of Achilles' shield. Yet Apollo, who here appears above the same shrine that Aeneas visited back in Book 3, drawing a bow and signaling victory of the gods and Roman armies over the Eastern threat, gives the Principate an almost mystical, cosmogonic foundation. Augustus is the man whom Fate foresaw for Rome from the very beginning. And on Octavian's head shines the same flame that miraculously appeared on the head of Ascanius during the fall of Troy.

Virgil organizes the passage into a veritable history of Ancient Rome, with plenty of nods to Livy's own *History*. The first scene depicted on the shield is of Romulus and Remus "suckling the udders" of the Capitoline wolf. Next comes the rape of the Sabine women and the wars that were fought as a result of the episode, the enemies therein described as particularly ferocious while "Aeneas's descendants fought for liberty." This is followed by episodes about the conflicts with the Etruscans, who attempted to restore their king to the Roman throne. Modern readers will recognize the legendary stories of Rome's origins, like the story of the virgin Cloelia, who escaped from the Etruscan Porsenna by swimming across the Tiber, or the geese that, with their honking, foiled a nighttime attack of the Gauls.

Then there is a startling description of two figures from more recent Roman history, who appear in hell on the shield. In Tartarus, Cataline is "hanging from a dangerous cliff, trembling before the Furies," while Cato—most likely the younger, though for a long time believed to be the Elder—is placed among the pious spirits, dispensing laws even in the afterlife.

At last we come to Caesar Augustus, shown leading the Romans in battle. The unmistakable marks of a god ("two flames shooting from his temples, and his father's star shines above his head") make him the man of destiny. In opposition to the Roman army advance the "Barbarian ranks" of Antony and "sacrilege! The Egyptian bride." This exclamation may allude to African Dido's marriage ambitions.

Virgil's verses then turn grave and fraught, as if the battle were a war of the worlds between Rome and the Orient. Sea creatures materialize on this side, "barking" Anubis on that. The Egyptians, Arabs, Indians, and Sabaeans (a Semitic people from the southern Arabian Peninsula) flee in fear of Apollo, while Cleopatra grows "pale with her future death."

In the end Augustus emerges victorious, returning to Rome to celebrate his triple triumph, cheered on by his citizens, who honor him with games and sacrifices. The defeated are taken prisoner and marched down the streets of the city.

> Seated at the threshold of the beautiful temple of Apollo, he accepts the gifts of the people and hangs them over the doors proudly; the vanquished peoples pass in a long parade, with their various tongues and dress and arms.
> (8.720-723)

This is the spectacle that Aeneas contemplates on his shield, a gift from his mother Venus. He is ignorant, *ignarus*, of what will become history, and he can't help but marvel at the shield. When he's ready, he takes that history upon his shoulder—*attolens umero*—just as he had once carried his father Anchises on his back.

Once again Aeneas will march on, but now it isn't the past he's carrying on his shoulders: This time he bears the weight of his fragile future.

* * *

Maybe that's what happened. Maybe Virgil didn't succeed in creating a here and now all that distinct from Homer. But an unforgettable afterlife? That he knew how to create. An afterlife that is, like squalor, easy to slide into. The hard part is getting back up.

. . . Goddess-born,
Anchises' son, the way to hell is easy,
the door to Dis is open night and day,
but to return, and climb out into the air,
that is the task, that is the hard labor.
(6. 125-129)

It's striking to reread Book 6 of the *Aeneid* now—or read it for the first time, if you didn't in school. These verses shrink whatever debt Virgil owes Homer and for which he's often criticized.

On the other hand, the debt owed Virgil by every writer that came after him skyrockets. Starting with Dante. Without Book 6 there would be no *Divine Comedy*. In fact, it was Virgil who first mapped the entire Underworld that would become the literary topos we all know today, a place of shadows, thorny bushes, howling dogs, ferrymen, tortured souls, and impalpable angelic spirits. Even if the first literary voyage to Hades—in Greek, *katabasis*, the descent to the bowels of the earth, or *nekyia*, the ritual in which ghosts were summoned to foretell the future—occurs in Books 10 and 11 of the *Odyssey*, when Ulysses meets Achilles, Agamemnon, Patroclus, and others, the *Aeneid* would remain an unparalleled masterpiece on the merits of Book 6 alone.

Because Aeneas doesn't just climb down to hell and stand there slack jawed. He proceeds with *pectore firmo*, "strong of heart." He wants to understand the criteria and laws to which the dead in Hades are subject. He keeps asking the Sibyl and the shadows he encounters to explain—just as Dante does on his educational journey as he makes his way toward Paradise with Virgil as his guide.

Reading Book 6 today, as we follow the footsteps of Aeneas and the Sibyl, we see Blake's illustrations of hell. As we encounter the fallen Trojans, we shiver at the sight of the triumph of the Black Death. As we enjoy beholding fearsome Dido, we hear the Baroque melodies of Bach and Handel.

One thing's for sure: we read on and we tremble.

The role Book 6 performs in the *Aeneid* has long been the subject of debate. Does it merely function as an interlude between the Odyssean and the Iliadic sections of the epic? (Aeneas visits the Underworld by himself, leaving his companions on the beaches of Cumae after the death of his helmsman Palinurus, who, lured by the God of Sleep, fell into the sea.) Or is it the part of the *Aeneid* in which Virgil is most free to follow his own poetic instincts, having set down the burden of Homeric tradition and the need to keep the plot going, and shows us the sum of his humanity?

Whatever the case, the effect is powerfully dystopian. The future awaiting Rome is glorious, yes, but it is described by a dead man in the realm of the dead as the work of people who have yet to be born, seen there in the form of ghosts. All the splendor that the Principate will herald, Aeneas learns about in the afterlife, underneath Lake Avernus, after passing through "the gaping rocky mouth of a deep cavern, / enclosed by a shadowy wood and dark lake / that no birds can fly over safely, such is the breath exhaled / from its black throat that rises to the sky" (6.237-241).

Having performed the rites at the temple of Apollo at Cumae and buried his friend Misenus as the god bid him, Aeneas and the possessed Sibyl *ibant oscuri sola sub nocte per umbra*, "went in the lonesome shade of night" (6.268).

After getting past the beds of Sorrow, Cares, Disease, Old Age, Fear, Hunger, Poverty, Labor, Death, "Death's brother" Sleep (the allusion is to drunkenness, probably, not repose), War, and Discord, the pair encounters the monsters that populate Hades in classical myth: the Chimaera, Gorgons, and Harpies.

At the threshold of the Underworld, where souls crowd around and beg to be taken to their eternal destiny, Aeneas is interrogated by the boatman Charon. The living are not allowed to enter the land of the dead, he says. Hercules, Orpheus, and Pirithous caused too much trouble when they crossed over. So Aeneas shows him the golden bough, the passport to the Underworld and a gift for Hades's wife Proserpine, which Aeneas had brought with him at the suggestion of the Sibyl:

> "Trojan Aeneas, known for valor and piety,
> descends into the shadows of Erebus to find
> his father there. If his devotion fails to move you,
> accept this bough." She drew the golden bough
> that she had kept hidden in her robe.
> (6.403-407)

And with that, the hero is allowed to board the boat to the Underworld, which "groaned beneath his weight, and was swamped with water"; the flesh and bones of the living weigh more than the souls of the dead, we read in Virgil, but we feel as though we are reading Dante.

Drugging Cerberus with a magic morsel of bread, Aeneas and the Sibyl contemplate the shadows of dead babies and suicides who, "hating the light of day," threw their lives away. Here is where Aeneas recognizes Dido, among those whom "love wasted away," those condemned to be tortured by matters of the heart beyond the grave. At the sight of the man she once loved, the woman responds with an *inimica*, "hostile" look and escapes to the Fields of Lamentation where she must wander forever with her husband Sychaeus.

Then comes the train of the war dead, where the hero re-encounters Trojans like Glaudias and Deiphobous, Hector's favorite brother, hideously disfigured by Helen when, Paris dead, she becomes his wife and betrays him by delivering him up to Menelaus. It is the infernal region of Tartarus, where the River Phlegethon flows, the seat for punishing the greatest sinners.

The Sibyl tells Aeneas that here live the Giants and Titans, Centaurs and Lapiths, as well as all those who betrayed their homelands or families, or hoarded their wealth, or ignored justice, or offended the gods. And many others still.

Had I a hundred tongues, a hundred mouths,
and a voice as strong as iron, I could not tell you
all the forms of their crimes or their punishments.
(6.625-627)

At last they deliver the golden bough to Proserpine and there appears before Aeneas the moving sight of Elysium. Here dwell the poets, priests, patriots, and those whose lives were guided by pietas, their heads wrapped in bandeaux. Here is where the founders of Troy spend eternity: "The same love of chariots / and arms when they were alive, the same care they took to train their horses, / survived down there, under the earth" (6.653-655).

Aeneas finally spots his father, standing apart from the others in a green vale, watching souls about to reemerge into the light and be reincarnated. Their meeting is filled with tears of joy, and Aeneas tries in vain to embrace his father, as he had tried to embrace Creusa: "Three times he tried to throw his arms around his father's neck, / three times the image escaped his grasp / as if it were a breeze or on the wings of sleep" (6.700-702).

After an eschatological section with Platonic underpinnings, in which Anchises explains to his son the universal designs and principles that regulate the metempsychosis of souls, the time has come for Aeneas to be happy. And discover Italy.

> Now I will tell you of the glory that awaits the Dardans,
> and of the Italian stock that will be descended from you,
> and the illustrious souls who will bear our name.
> Of all this I will tell you, and show you your fate.
> (6.756-759)

One by one Anchises points out Aeneas's descendants, who will bring glory to Rome. The first is his son, who, he is told, will rule over Alba Longa. (This must be a different son, a son the hero will have with Lavinia. It seems unlikely that he is referring to Ascanius/Iulus, since the city of Alba Longa has yet to be founded. This might be the most serious oversight among the hundred or so that litter the *Aeneid*.)

After the line of Alban kings, the soul of Romulus steps forward. Romulus will build noble Rome on the seven hills, the city whose "empire will stretch across the earth and whose soul reach heaven." Paul Veyne argues that the Latin word *animos* (soul) should here be translated as "pride." Last comes the crux of Anchises's prophecy:

This is the man who has been promised to you,
Augustus Caesar, the son of the Divine,
who shall restore a golden age to Latium,
in fields where Saturn ruled, and his empire
will extend to the Garamantes and Indians.
(6.791-795)

Aeneas listens to his father enumerate Augustus's military victories, which will extend his dominion into Africa and the Orient and "beyond the zodiac." This is followed by an excursus, in chronological order, of Romulus's successors, the rest of the seven kings—Numa Pompilius, whose premature gray hair is a symbol of wisdom; the warrior Tullus Hostilius; Ancus Marcius, whom Anchises criticizes as a populist, though we have little information in that regard; and the three Tarquin kings, Tarquinius Priscus, Servius Tullius, and Tarquinius Superbus—on down to the foundation of the S.P.Q.R.

Next comes a list of the heroes of the Republic: the Decii, the Drusi (the line of Augustus's wife Livia Drusilla), Torquatus, Camillus, until the civil bloodshed between Caesar and Pompey. Anchises warns, "Do not let civil war be your custom, sons, / do not take up arms against the vitals of your own land" (6.832-833).

Still others line up to be born. Cato the Elder, the Gracchi, Scipio Africanus and Scipio Emilianus—the first declared victory at Zama, the second razed Carthage to the ground—Gaius Atilius Regulus, and Quintus Fabius Maximus, who wore down Hannibal by a strategy of delay called *cunctando*. All of a sudden the triumphal tone is interrupted.

Virgil slips in a sad reference to Augustus's nephew, the son of his sister Octavia, who died prematurely after being adopted by the emperor in 25 BC and appointed his successor. The reference, it must be said, is sycophantic and deceptive; the only justification for bringing up the boy is that he shares a name with Marcus Claudius Marcellus, who defeated the Gauls at Clastidium in 222 BC. When the boy died, the *princeps* declared an extended period of mourning in the city and in his name completed construction of the Theater of Marcellus, which had begun under Caesar, in the southern part of Campus Martius, by demolishing the other buildings in the area, including a temple to Pietas.

Virgil toes the imperial line, calling Marcellus a "beautiful young man in shining armor" who bears a resemblance to the chosen *puer* in Eclogue IV, only here the boy's eyes are downcast and his face dark. Supposedly, when Octavia read the passage, she became so overwhelmed with grief that she fainted. And the ignoramuses of history have read into this passage the coming of Jesus Christ.

In the end, time flies in paradise too. Once Anchises has foretold the wars and labors that will take place in Latium, the hero hurries to climb back out into the light. He has been presented with the future of Rome, a future yet to be borne out as per these words:

> Romans, remember to govern the people.
> That is your art; to bring peace with laws,
> spare the conquered, and crush the proud.
> (6.851-853)

The Gates of Dreams

As the saying goes, be careful what you wish for; it might just come true. When Virgil describes in the *Aeneid* the future glory that attends Rome under the aegis of Augustus, a good part of that future has already come to pass. And it is not as glorious as he had hoped.

If Virgil believed in Augustus's project, it was not because he was forced at gunpoint, but because he needed to believe in something and someone. Just like everybody else. When he lost faith, he did not disavow or insult the person he had believed in. He chose to preserve the memory of a time when he could claim to have been happy—the years immediately following the Battle of Actium in 31 BC up to the suspicious death of his friend Cornelius Gallus in 26 BC—in such a way that no one could sully it.

Five years. That's it. That's how long Virgil could call himself an Augustan poet. That is the period when the *Aeneid* is written—or nailed—down. After that, silence. There is no trace in the *Aeneid* of the events that took place after and leading up to Virgil's death in 19 BC, a period in which he never stopped writing. Not a nod to the progression of Augustus's Principate, not a reference to the definitive dismantling of the republic, not a hint of the growing tensions over the succession to the throne of Rome.

Maybe Virgil was shocked. Maybe he was left speechless. Or maybe, just like his Aeneas, he didn't want to concede and be forced to acknowledge that he had been wrong to believe. Maybe he didn't want to have to admit that the golden age that Rome had been anxiously awaiting was no more than a pipe dream—because the reality was turning out to be a nightmare.

Besides, at a certain point Augustus began writing about all that he had accomplished in his life and no longer needed to wait for Virgil's *Aeneid*. It would become the *Res Gestae Divi Augusti*, or the Deeds of the Divine Augustus, a detailed index of everything he had done and a very interesting work of literature for defying categorization and for the fascinating destinies of its engraved copies. According to the will of the emperor, after his death the *Res Gestae* was to be inscribed in bronze and placed in front of his mausoleum, near the Ara Pacis, for the public to see.

In the *Aeneid* Virgil availed himself of the subtle advantage of his elegance. If he ever had any disappointments or regrets, they all shine through in two passages—but their emergence is indistinct, minor, private, almost dreamlike in form. The city of Actium, also mentioned in some of the prophecies, makes a marked appearance in Book 3, the most problematic book in the entire poem, in which the meaning of a whole verse, line 340, is missing, perhaps a sign that it was written (or rewritten) after the overarching structure of the epic was in place.

On their voyage to Latium, the Trojans sail past the kingdom of the detested Ulysses and drop anchor near the promontory of Actium, in western Greece. After making sacrifices to Jupiter and other gods, the exiles honor fallen Troy with a celebration of games, which from then on will be called Actian games, after the city Actium. At the time of Aeneas, Actium must have been little more than a *parva urbs*, a small village, yet the hero decides to leave a shield of hollow brass there for posterity, with the inscription "Aeneas Offers These Arms Taken from the Conquering Greeks" (3.288). Ever since, Actium, which nearly a thousand years on will see Octavian defeat Antony and Cleopatra, has been named Nicopolis, or the "City of Victory."

This emphasis on placing large hopes in small, almost trivial symbols happens again a little later in Book 3. Aeneas and his fleet next stop on the shores of Buthrotum, in present-day Albania, near the border with Greece. Here reigns Andromache, who, having been set free—she was enslaved after the death of Hector—married Helenus. The couple has reconstructed a miniature Troy on the beach, which Aeneas spies (3.349-51):

On our approach I see a humbler Troy,
a simulation of the towering Pergamus,

a little stream that they call Xanthus,
and kiss the entrance of a Scaean Gate.

Andromache and Helenus can't have reconstructed
a scaled-down model of their ancient birthplace just to
assuage the homesickness they feel as refugees. These verses
raise several questions, in fact, about the ambiguity of the
mission that Aeneas is about to embark on. In this city, his
purpose appears almost oxymoronic.

The innate paradox of the Penates, the household gods
which Hector's shade entrusts to Aeneas as Troy is going up
in smoke, is brought to bear in this big-small dynamic. The
Penates represent rootedness to a specific social, political,
and cultural identity; they are not interchangeable statuettes
that can be easily transferred from one political institution to
another, which begs the question: what can the founding of
Rome and its famed destiny mean if it will not be governed by
the pact that the city shall remain true to its values forever?

Virgil seems to be suggesting that we should not seek glory
in grandeur, if grandeur means distorting Fate. Instead, we
should be true to who we are, to what we believe. That's the
only way we can we say we're fully satisfied, like Andromache
and Helenus, who live in a city that, though smaller and
poorer than Troy, shares the same fundamental values:

Be happy, your fortune has been made.
We are called by one fate, then another,
But you have found repose.
(3.493-495)

* * *

Before concluding this chapter, let's return a moment to Book 6, where we last left Aeneas.

Apparently, it's not so hard to find your way out of the Underworld after all, despite what the Sibyl said. It is impossible, however, to remember what you saw there.

> There are two gates of Sleep, one made of horn
> through which true shades depart this place easily;
> the other is made of polished ivory and shines.
> But through that gate the Dead send up false dreams.
> And as Anchises tells them these things, he ushers
> his son and the Sibyl to the ivory gate.

The description of the two gates of Dreams (*Aeneid*, 6.893-900) may have been lifted verbatim from the *Odyssey* (19.562-567), but more troubling for generations of readers is where Anchises, after having gone to great lengths to describe the future of Rome, leads his son: through the portal of false dreams.

What can I say? It's just a handful of lines, a passing reference unrelated to the main plot. Does it have no symbolic significance, as some scholars propose? Can we chalk it up to an irrelevant misprint? While we're on the subject, is there such a thing as a completely true or a completely false dream?

This much is clear: Once he goes through the gate of false dreams, Aeneas loses all memory of his father's words. From the following book, Book 7, to the end of the epic, the hero reacts to all the events that Fate subjects him to with genuine surprise. Aeneas forgets all about Anchises's prophecy, he retains nothing. But the reader doesn't forget what's awaiting the hero on his march to Rome.

Given Virgil's precise wording, we are more than justified if we ask ourselves what the point of Book 6 is. What's the purpose of stopping in the middle of the poem to tack on nine hundred lines about oracles from the Underworld if the protagonist is going to forget what he learned the moment he comes back out into the light? If an unequivocal answer is not provided in the *Aeneid*—which will not make the slightest mention of Anchises's predictions again—it seems plausible to think that passing through that ivory gate was less in the interests of Aeneas than it was in the interests of the poet.

Virgil is the one who believed he could reach out and touch the golden age before realizing he had crossed over into a world of lies. It was not among true shades that the poet experienced peace, concord, and serenity—or at least got a moment of respite. Never mind, Virgil seems to be saying, while he and Aeneas are rudely transported back to reality. He has no intention of erasing his dream, even if it is false, even if now he is gripping not the resplendent golden age that he had hoped for but an age of rusted iron.

7
OTHERS, ERGO OURSELVES:
ITALY AND THE ITALIC PEOPLES IN THE *AENEID*

From the scorched hill
listen to the cry of the lost.
Nothing is left of them
but a blackened mound
with smashed altars, a veil
singed and torn in two.
Listen to the lament of mortals,
nocturnal men with no temple;
no one built them
the safety of walls and architraves.
Listen. The scorched
foundations are crying out; the last
plank is being ripped from the walls,
and as it calls to you
cleaves and splits apart.
On your walls,
breaking them up into confused wails,
saxifrage spreads its roots.
—GIORGIO MANGANELLI, *Juvenilia, III, Poems*

I will never forget the time, September of my first year
in high school, when our teacher asked the class: "Have
you ever wondered why, in the span of a century, Greece

gave birth to philosophy, math, history, law, geometry, architecture, medicine, and a lot else besides, while the rest of the world was busy howling in the woods and wearing blue face paint?"

I am perfectly aware that this somewhat simple question, worded for the express purpose of getting the attention of a group of students who knew nothing and had just returned from summer break, doesn't hold up to the scrutiny of sociologists and anthropologists or meet the standards of politically correct speech. Yet it is a question that I still ask myself today whenever I visit Athens, Delphi, Epidaurus, and Magna Graecia, or eagerly scan the verses of a comedy by Aristophanes, or read the preamble of one of Demosthenes's speeches: Why *there* and not elsewhere? Is there a connection between geography and culture? Not to inconvenience Kenneth White's theory of geopoetics, according to which there is a strong correlation between artistic creation and one's surroundings, but is it really possible for place to shape the way we think and for the way we think to shape place? If it is clear that Hellenic blue skies don't make us more intelligent—though definitely more cheerful and maybe more creative—what connections exist between the poetry of an entire country and its geography?

I can't hide the fact that my need to figure this problem out has long been tied to a sense of pride in my origins, a pride that never abated during my years as a student. On the contrary, with each new discovery my pride grew. I have never known how to answer that ingenuous question without dredging up—as one should—ideological and temporal relativism. But it has brought me no small comfort to know that, by birth and education, I am descended from those who invented knowledge while the rest of the western world was still "primitive." My country isn't called the Bel Paese for nothing, nor is it by chance that Italians are known as a population of poets.

Then, in recent months, the *Aeneid* arrived—or returned, rather. And how great and stinging was my surprise to read, right there in black and white, that until Aeneas landed on the coasts of Latium, we—I mean Italy and all of Europe, with the exception of Greece—were also, metaphorically speaking, busy shrieking at shrubs and painting our faces blue.

Because, in the *Aeneid*, we are not the good, the educated, the well-mannered, the refined. *We* are the others.

Between Topos and Toponymy: Italy in the Aeneid

> The Dawn had just begun to turn purple
> and chase away the stars, when in the distance
> we saw the dark hills and plains of Italy.
> Achates saw it first and cried "Italy!"
> "Italy!" the crew cried out with joy.
> (3.521-525)

Aeneas and the Trojan sailors first catch sight of Italy off the coast of Otranto, in Castrum Minervae to be precise, and we seem to share in the excitement of their "joyful cry." Maybe we even cheer along.

Unlike the *Iliad* and the *Odyssey*, the *Aeneid* isn't set in far-flung places that only a select few are fortunate enough to visit. Virgil's epic largely unfolds in Italy. Aeneas is marching straight for our backyard. And yet we're seldom aware of the fact that every day we plough the same turf that Virgil's hero ploughed almost three thousand years ago.

Italians rarely puff out their chests and proclaim, "Aeneas was here." At least I've never heard anyone say that. There are no ancient monuments to the hero, modern monuments are in short supply, and even in contemporary iconography—with the exception of educational TV programs—Aeneas is overshadowed by Homer's world-famous immortal heroes. In spite of the fact that our protagonists do not travel through remote or mythic places—there are no remote Fortunate Isles, no mysterious caves at the edge of the world where nymphs reside, no bizarre civilizations of lotus eaters—the geography of Virgil vanishes the minute we close the book. The only place names that a reader can recall are those for which the poet takes pains to provide an origin story, like Caieta, so named for his nurse, or Cape Misenum and Palinurus, named for two fellow travelers lost at sea.

If, in classical geography, all roads lead to Rome, the *Aeneid* is no exception. In fact, the Caput Mundi is practically the only place that Virgil describes accurately and in detail, down to its temples and monuments—in some cases, with the meticulousness of a roadmap. Otherwise, the *Aeneid*'s depiction of Italy is rather cryptic and evanescent. Even when we can pinpoint an exact location, doubts linger.

Those doubts stem not only from the epic's long lists of cities and civilizations—modeled after Homer's catalog of ships—which can leave readers bewildered. But, even when we can locate the Rutulians on the coast of Latium around Ardea, it is highly unlikely that no one other than a leading historian and scholar of ancient geography will recognize their direct ancestors in names like Massicus, Abas, Asilas, Astyr, Cunaro, Cupavo, Ocnes, Aulestes, and others (for the complete list of kings allied with Mezentius, see verses 163-218 of Book 10).

The alienating effect of space in the *Aeneid* comes from Virgil's disinterest in describing topoi, or "actual places," as per the primary meaning of the Greek word τόπος, in the epic. Virgil's topoi are closer to "commonplaces," rhetorical conventions—the secondary translation of the Greek word. The cities, ports, mountains, seas, woods, rivers, and plains that dot the *Aeneid* allow the poet to spread out the epic material with which to enchant his readers; every place referenced in the poem is a function of the mythological story that he is given to tell.

So, for instance, a modest sulfur spring near Tibur, which also earns mention in Horace's *Odes*, in the *Aeneid* is turned into "a sacred fountain / that roars in deep Albunea, greatest of all forests, / and expels mephitic vapors in its shade" (7.83-84). A remote spot in the mountains of Irpinia, near Rocca San Felice, a small town in the province of Avellino, is described as "famously sung in many lands." This is the valley of the River Ansanto—a roaring brook in the epic, in real life a stream no deeper than a few feet.

Finally, of the five cities in Latium that Juno incites

to take up arms against Aeneas, no fewer than three have presented critics since antiquity with several problems. Virgil calls them *magnae urbes*, but only Tibur and Ardea could be accurately described as small centers of modest importance at the time. Certainly Atina, Amtemna, and Crustumerium could not be. (According to sources, Crustumerium had already fallen into decline and disappeared by the fourth century BC.) The epithets Virgil gives them also appear bewilderingly inflated. Maybe Tibur did merit the name "the lofty," given its elevated position, but why is Atina, now a small municipality in the province of Frosinone, called "the powerful"? It's a safe bet that *turrigerae* Amtemna had not turrets.

And why five cities, anyway? Why not more? Or fewer? Is he alluding to the first contingent in Homer's catalog of ships, the Boeotians, which opens with five captains? If so, why that particular reference? These and many other questions about the toponomy of the *Aeneid* are destined to remain unanswered.

Every place that Virgil mentions opens up a laundry list of possible literary references—and equally long is the list of issues that remain unresolved. If, therefore, the majority of the epithets related to geography are to be read as entirely decorative, should we infer that Virgil is lying or being deceptive when he describes Italy? Or, worse, that he considered Italy to be historically and aesthetically inferior to the landscapes of Greece, and therefore thought it necessary to prettify the country with myths and exaggerate the features of its locales?

No, Virgil didn't need to make things up in order to

embellish Italy; its natural splendors were plain to anyone with eyes to see. Especially the eyes of a man who had already sung about the beauty of Italy in the *Eclogues* and *Georgics*. But what Virgil held dear, as a human and a poet, was recounting the beauty of an unspoiled, simple, rustic, and natural Italy—not unlike the Mantua he was born and raised in. The *Aeneid* is an ode to the land "before" and a stark contrast to the "after" in which Virgil and his readers lived.

What we have here is a popular ode to a pure Italy, an Italy with no capital cities, only suburbs and outskirts, before the Roman metropolis reared its arrogant head. Virgil's nostalgia is completely political and ideological. Make no mistake: The poet was not an ecologist ahead of his time nor an advocate of degrowth as the key to happiness (he was more of an expert in unhappiness).

In treating the geography of Italy in the *Aeneid*, Virgil mourns the loss of a country he could call his own; that's what makes it so beautiful and precious. Like Aeneas, he would have loved to say of Rome: "Here is my country, this is home."

In short, no one should go looking for Virgil's Italy on maps, be they actual maps or world mythology maps. Perhaps Virgil's Italy exists only in dreams—in dreams that have been dashed.

* * *

In Book 8, Virgil provides a curious etymology for Latium. As he has it, the name means "refuge, hiding place" from the Latin verb *latere,* "to hide" (not to be confused with the noun *latus*, for "flank, side"). Virgil doesn't neglect to make up a poetic archaeology of places in Italy that will one day become Roman. Latium takes its name from Saturn, who ushers in a golden age on earth when he seeks a hiding place (hence the name of the region) in Rome after being stripped of his powers by Jupiter and by the thirst for power he inspired in mankind.

This is how Latium first appears to Aeneas, from his ship:

> From the sea Aeneas saw a great forest
> across which cut the beautiful flowing Tiber
> whose eddying waters, shining with golden sands,
> poured into the sea. Above and around him
> birds of all colors, the kinds of birds
> that hover around rivers and riverbanks,
> were stroking the air, filling the forest with song.
> (7.29-35)

It isn't hard to see, especially for those who have felt frustrated by the neglected state of Rome today, that Virgil resorts to using a literary topos to describe the place, the poetic convention of *locus amoenus*, beloved by Alexandrian poetry. Latium as described in the *Aeneid* more closely resembles Calypso's pristine island (which for nearly three millennia Homer scholars have struggled to locate) than the urban landscapes that now extend from Rome to the Tyrrhenian. Indeed, the Tiber in the *Aeneid* is called *fluvio Tibernius amoeno*—"the beautiful flowing Tiber."

Shortly after the exiles land on Latium's coast, Virgil

recounts the fulfillment of the Harpy's prophecy in Book 3. According to the prophecy, the Trojans would know they had at last arrived at their destination when, upon reaching a strange beach, they would be so famished that they would eat the tables on which they lunched. The poet narrates the episode with a levity that seems out of character. Relieved at having arrived in Latium, father and son are captured in a lighthearted scene that takes the drama out of the malicious bird's omen—and gives the lines an unexpected sweetness.

Caught up in the moment, Ascanius bites into the crust of his bread, the shape of which reminds him of a table, and exclaims *adludens* (playfully): "Look! We're eating our tables too!" (7.116). And here Virgil rewards readers with what in my opinion is one of the most beautiful phrases in the entire poem. Recognizing the word that signals the end of their toils, the smiling hero doesn't say anything in response, but instead "snatche[s] [the word] from his son's lips and shield[s] it" (7.119). The hero's love for his son is one of the abiding emotional themes in the epic.

Then, with great tenderness and enormous relief, Aeneas speaks up:

> "Hail! Land the fates promised!
> Hail! You faithful gods of Troy!
> This is our home. Here is our country."
> (7.120-122)

Aeneas addresses Italy directly—"hail," he calls to it, hoping for the best. He calls the place "our country." He calls it "home." It doesn't matter if Fate will soon force him to see "globs of blood" shed and trample over "blood mingled with rage." At the moment he is spellbound to behold the beauty of Italy for the first time, with the same sense of awe that must fill the eyes of children born today at Fatebenefratelli, the hospital in Rome where the windows at the maternity ward still open onto the enchanting Tiber Island.

We, the Italic Peoples

In Book 8 of the *Aeneid*, Evander, the Arcadian king who settled in Italy and fathered a son, ill-starred Pallas, shows Aeneas the citadel on the Palatine that he himself founded. On this same site, many years later, Romulus will place the first stone of Rome.

Then the king describes the people who populated Latium long ago:

> These woods were once inhabited by native fauns
> and nymphs, and by a race of men who were born
> from the trunks of oak trees. They had no laws
> or culture. They didn't know how to yoke their oxen,
> or how to sow their crops, or store their harvests.
> They lived off wild fruits and what they hunted.
> (8. 314-319)

At the time in which the events of the *Aeneid* unfold, the Italic peoples who descended from these primitive ancestors had by then learned the secrets of farming and husbandry and the principles of law and religion. Yet their temperaments still ran from hot-blooded to cold-hearted. Aeneas couldn't have found a place where he felt more like an outsider than he does in Italy. And the Italic peoples couldn't regard the new arrival with greater suspicion than they do.

Nothing could be further from the rules of hospitality laid out by the Greeks than the reaction in Latium to the Trojans' arrival. Sure, Aeneas and his comrades are immediately and warmly welcomed by the Latin king, but otherwise the hero triggers nothing short of collective hysteria. On one side are the allies of the Latins who literally jockey to align themselves with Aeneas. Today we wouldn't think twice to say that they jump on the proverbial bandwagon. Even more insulting, at this point in the *Aeneid*, the hero hasn't even won yet. "Many peoples ally themselves with the Trojan hero and his name spreads far and wide in Latium" (8.13-14): It's almost as if there isn't a king who, for reasons of old age or long-ago prophecies or a lack of heirs, does not see Aeneas as a strongman to whom they should hand over their thrones and all their subjects.

We have already mentioned the predicament that Latinus creates by offering Aeneas his daughter's hand in marriage, then and there, even though Aeneas never asked for it. Latin's daughter is betrothed to Turnus, a man favored by Queen Amata, and the queen—as we have already said—will be furious at this slight to her would-be son-in-law and hatch a war that will embroil all Latium. On the other side are the allies of Turnus, who, blinded by anger, like wild horses, immediately set to conspiring against Aeneas: "All souls were rattled, and all of Latium / stirred with alarming tumult, and the wild youth / were enraged" (8.4-6). That is to say nothing of the alliances and hostilities among the various tribes that turn the whole length of Italy, from north to south, into a minefield.

In short, as soon as he steps foot in Latium, a bewildered Aeneas finds himself staring at a landscape whose beauty is beyond dispute, but such is the political circus that he almost longs for the orderly ranks of tribes, neatly divided, each with its own banner, on the plains of Troy. No sooner has Aeneas got his bearings than he is taking up arms: "Italy, once tranquil and undisturbed, was on fire" (7.624). What can we say? It isn't the warmest of welcomes nor the fuzziest of welcoming committees.

Juno may decide that "there has been enough of fear and deception," but that doesn't mean the Italic peoples have the means necessary to declare war. Quite the contrary.

Only Turnus—the one Homeric hero in the *Aeneid*, as we saw in the chapter on Fate—is prepared to fight: "He cried out / for his arms and searched his bed and halls for them; what broke forth in him was / a lust for battle, the crazy curse of war, / and fury" (7. 460-462). Before the decisive battle with Aeneas, the king of the Rutulians is compared to a bull, testing "the ire of his horns against a tree" and tearing up the earth with his hoofs. But we can't be sure that the other men have the same warring determination—nor even, alas, the same *physique du role*; elsewhere Virgil describes the Italic peoples as "lazy and unaccustomed to war."

But it would be best to hear from Virgil's Italic peoples

themselves (9.601-20) about who they are and what they value:

> What god, what madness made you come to Italy?
> You won't find sons of Atreus here, or liars
> like Ulysses. We come from hardy stock
> and dunk our babies in ice-cold rivers to inure them
> to the bitter cold. Our boys are up at dawn
> hunting and rambling through the woods. For sport
> they break horses and shoot arrows. Our youth
> work hard and learn to live on little, taming
> the land with rakes and laying siege to cities.
> No age group is exempt from bearing arms.
> We prod our oxen with the back-ends of our spears.
> Old age doesn't dampen our spirits or vigor.
> We cover our gray hair with our helmets,
> gorge on new prey and subsist on plunder.
> But you, in your saffron-colored and deep purple
> clothes, you love luxury, you like to dance,
> you wear tunics with long fancy sleeves
> and decorate your headgear with ribbons.
> You're not Trojan men, you're Trojan women.
> Go back to Mount Dindymus! The double
> flute is playing the sound that people like you
> listen to. Your tambourines are calling!
> The flute of your Mother Goddess is calling you!
> Put down your swords and leave the fighting to men.

In the *Aeneid* it is Numanus, Turnus's brother-in-law, who draws a clear line between "you Greeks" and "we Italic peoples" as he inveighs against the Trojan soldiers, words that Ascanius will answer with an arrow, signaling the boy's initiation into battle. Numanus pulls no punches: He mocks

Aeneas's comrades for being constantly besieged, *bis capti*, Troy having been captured twice, first by Heracles and then by Agamemnon. But it is not their record on the battlefield so much as their Greek model of education and culture that comes in for the Italic peoples' disdain, culminating in the offensive, boorish feminization of the other.

Numanus takes great pride in illustrating how Italic youths are raised, learning to "live on little," toiling in the soil or attacking and looting neighboring villages. Every stage of life is taken up with the fanatic exercise of war, a duty not even the elders are excused from. Everyone in Italy, including the gray and balding, dons a helmet. The description of the Italic lifestyle is generally based on the example of the hardworking and frugal Latin farmer, who neither covets wealth nor entertains pipe dreams, according to the model of the *civis romanus*, who lives humbly and follows the code of *mos maiorum*, previously sung about by Quintus Ennius. The lines also contain numerous echoes of the *Georgics* about the effort needed to cultivate "hard" land.

What is striking about the words of Numanus is the stark contrast between Greek culture and Roman culture: Whereas the former is soft and accustomed to creature comforts, the latter is no-nonsense and burly. The Greeks carry flutes and drums, gifts of the Cybele that signify the arts and poetry. The Romans brandish spears and knives, and have neither the time nor the patience for knowledge.

In the *Aeneid*, this clash of two ways of seeing—and imparting—the world is already present in Anchises' prophecy. In the afterlife (6.847-50) he urges Aeneas not to forget that the aim of the Romans is to dominate the world, not excel in the arts:

> Others, I believe, will sculpt with greater elegance
> and fashion living faces from stone, and plead
> cases in courts of law with greater eloquence,
> describe with greater skill the wheeling motion
> of the stars and mark the moment of their rising.

Sadly, it's too late for me to go back to school and tell my teacher all that the *Aeneid* enshrines with searing clarity. The lines above make clear that those "elegant" peoples who dedicate their time to sculpture, oratory, and astronomy are Greek. While *we*, as Numanus says, "come from hardy stock" and are descended from kids who wandered around the fields prodding cattle like a posse of cowboys. In spite of that, our goal remains the same: to govern the world.

Aeneas will soon unite with these people—our people, our ancestors—to produce the modern race from which all Europeans, excluding those lucky souls born in Athens and soothed by the singing of the Muses, descend. Not only are the founding of Rome and the later fortunes of the empire at play in the *Aeneid*; as we shall see, Virgil almost unintentionally succeeds in narrating the integration of Greek measure and proportion with Latin impetuousness and ardor, which will give rise to the first account of the Mediterranean character in the history of literature.

Because the first brick laid at the end of the epic does not belong to Rome; that won't occur until many centuries after Aeneas defeats the Rutulians. What the last verse of the *Aeneid* lays down are the foundations of human nature.

* * *

Allowing that the *Aeneid* is a patriotic poem, as some argue, we still need to recognize that there is nothing Roman about its conclusion. After two thousand years of Virgil studies, I feel confident that I am not spoiling things by revealing that the epic about the foundation of Rome does not actually end with the foundation of Rome. More importantly, there is no happy ending for the reader.

Book 12 of the *Aeneid* ends with the sword of Aeneas being plunged into Turnus's chest—that's it. Rome is still just a glint in his eye. Virgil's hero hesitates before murdering the king of the Rutulians in cold blood, as the king pleads for his life and appeals to the memory of Aeneas's father Anchises. Actually, Aeneas stays his hand until he catches sight of the "fatal baldric" glittering on Turnus's side—the studded leather belt that the king had taken from Pallas after brutally murdering him and desecrating his body. The memory of "cruel sorrow" prompts Aeneas to strike the final blow and avenge the unjustified killing of the boy.

The last two verses go like this: "Turnus's limbs froze and fell slack / and with a groan his indignant life fled to the shades."

Vitaque cum gemitu fugit indignata sub umbras.

The power of this last line has resonated with Virgil's readers for centuries, and to this day that resonance has been accompanied by doubts about the line itself. For one, these are the exact same words used in Book 11, verse 831, to describe the death of the Amazon Camilla, Queen of the Volscians, when she is killed by the Etruscan Arruns. Along with the difficulty of translating the line—it is unclear why the poet uses the preposition *sub* ("under"), which complicates a literal translation, "under the shades," since there is no place lower than the kingdom of the dead—the search for a symbolic meaning to illuminate this cryptic and bleak ending has exasperated readers from the moment the epic first appeared. If Virgil's decision to conclude the *Aeneid* this way can be explained as a borrowing from Homer, his effort seems a little forced, resulting in a conclusion that feels truncated, nervous, almost incomplete.

Surely the petitions of Turnus come from the *Iliad*, when Hector begs Achilles to return his corpse to the Trojans so that he can receive a proper burial, while the appeal to fatherly love echoes Priam's plea to Achilles. Yet unlike Hector, Turnus has yet to be mortally wounded. It's unclear whether Turnus is pleading for his mortal remains or for his life. Aeneas seems to respond to the latter, seeing as the funerary rites never come up.

During my research, Paul Veyne—who explains away pious Aeneas's violent outburst as a "feature of local color" with no religious or philosophical significance—made me wonder whether this is Aeneas's first "cross-bred" act, whether the final flare-up, so at odds with the hyper-restraint that the hero has exhibited up until this point, with his nearly obsessive resolve to carry on despite everything and everyone, is the result of the commingling of the Greeks and Latins then underway. In other words, how can this irrational furor and fit of feeling in someone who has always been guided by pietas, including and especially in times of difficulty, be explained if not by a change in his character? If not by his having naturally adapted to the spirit of Latium, this new land?

The brutal murder of Turnus fails to move or shock; readers actually breathe a sigh of relief after the barbarities perpetrated by the king of the Rutulians over the course of the epic. His death at Aeneas's hand is not a function of the epic structure, either, though it does add a dramatic and theatrical flair to the epic's ending.

If we want to read this passage as the termination of the dispute over Lavinia, the woman claimed by both Aeneas and Turnus, then the duel between Paris and Menelaus in the *Iliad* does not bear comparison. There is much more than a woman at stake here: there's an empire. In Homer the political status of the Greeks and Trojans is unchanged by poem's end; the protagonists remain anchored to their prewar social positions. Troy falls and no one is compensated or promoted. There is only sorrow to go around. In Virgil, on the other hand, Aeneas gets dominion over Latium and settles his people into a political structure so new as to change their national identity. No one is what he was, no one can call themselves Trojan anymore. Aeneas goes from being a refugee to the king of a foreign land.

In dramatic terms, Aeneas doesn't even enjoy what might be called his moment of glory at the end of the *Aeneid*. The hero isn't seeking personal revenge, and the

Rutulians are certainly not the first group of people who have done damage to his life—and his family—which fell to pieces with the citadel of Troy. Far less is Virgil interested in rewarding the tears which his hero has shed for twelve long books with a surge of brute virility. The *Aeneid* is not a Hollywood blockbuster where the nerd finally morphs into a brave superhero; author and audience were not a maniple of idiots.

At the end of the poem, Aeneas does what he has always done: hesitates, stumbles, and weeps—only now, this once, for the first time, he experiences the thrill of following his instincts instead of humbly bowing to the rationality of preordained plans. Because we are no longer in Troy, we are now in Latium, a country destined to become Roman by, first and foremost, becoming Trojan—what is about to emerge is Rome, and with Rome, a people, and that people cannot be the same who were woefully defeated by Ulysses's horse.

Please don't misunderstand me. I don't mean that Virgil intended to plant a murder at the base of his *urbe* or turn the *Aeneid* into a bildungsroman in which the protagonist goes from being an honest man to a coldblooded killer over the course of the story. I will limit myself to observing how, much to my amazement, Aeneas is pious from the first to the penultimate line of the *Aeneid*. In the last line, he sheds his shatterproof Greek aplomb and becomes, at last, Mediterranean, and therefore human, just like the rest of us.

Taking the Aeneid *Back from the Fascists*

Just as, at the end of the epic, the soul of Turnus "indignantly" flees to the shades, the entire *Aeneid* indignantly
fled from the manipulation of the Fascists in Italy—while
Virgil was back in Naples rolling over in his grave. Not
only is it striking—or shocking—that the Fascist regime
willfully distorted the verses of the *Aeneid* into a weapon
of propaganda. What makes our heads spin is not so much
the intellectual malice but the blind ignorance behind their
operation.

Frankly, Fascism understood nothing about the *Aeneid*.

Unfortunately, the regime's sinister effect on classical
studies is still far from over. To this day the determination
with which Mussolini and others exploited and misrepre-
sented the meaning of the classical world, Ancient Rome
in particular, demands we point out certain textual truths
for a long overdue "defascistization" of the concept of
Greekness and Romanness. Beginning with Virgil and the
Aeneid.

Mussolini made his first public reference to ancient
Rome in a speech given in Trieste on September 20, 1920.
On the occasion, along with the usual paeans to the Italian
identity of Trieste and to Gabriele D'Annunzio's stature
as a poet, the public heard for the first time the whys
and wherefores that would quickly lead to what Luciano
Canfora calls Fascism's "Romanolatry": that Italy sprang
directly from Imperial Rome and therefore was obliged to
conquer the rest of the world and silence all opponents. You
can clearly see the sloppiness with which Fascist theorists

clung to—and canceled out—over a thousand years of historical dynamics, dynamics far more complex than the clichéd family tree foisted on the masses that claimed Italians were the direct descendants of the Quirites, as if the latter were their own grandparents.

Very soon this mania for the Roman world, which had become mistakenly synonymous with the Italian world, proved a founding plank of Fascist propaganda, involving gestures, symbols, and ceremonies that drew on superficial and deceptive understandings of classical iconography. It's worth remembering that there was nothing historically Roman about the so-called Roman salute: Extending one's arm to express allegiance to Fascism began with the legionaries of Fiume, themselves inspired by the film *Cabiria*, directed in 1914 by Giovanni Pastrone with the collaboration of D'Annunzio.

At no stage in history does a classical text, Greek or Roman, mention the gesture, nor is there a single work of art—not a painting, not a sculpture, not a coin—that depicts it. On the contrary, among ancient societies, including but not limited to those in the Mediterranean, gestures with the right hand (*dextera* in Latin) meant the opposite of what the Fascists took them to mean: They stood for friendship, peace, solidarity. Just look at the equestrian monument to Marcus Aurelius, now in the Capitoline Museums, where the emperor is shown raising his right arm, his hand relaxed, loose, his fingers pointing upward in a sign of universal respect. Mussolini even named Fascist paramilitary units after their Roman military counterparts (cohorts, legions, centurions) in an attempt, common to all dictatorships, to legitimize that which can't be legitimized, distorting history in order to create a set of rituals that falsely claim to be in keeping with the past.

No less disturbing are Mussolini's claims that the movement would restore to the present the glories of the past that Romulus set in motion, intended not only to evoke the splendors of ancient Rome but to suggest that Fascism was its reincarnation. Here are the Duce's exact words, on April 21, 1922: "Much of the immortal spirit of Rome is reborn in Fascism: The lictor is Roman, our organization of combat is Roman, our pride and our courage are Roman. *Civis romanus sum.*"

The definitive act occurred in 1924, when, on Mussolini's orders, the celebration of the birth of Rome on April 21 replaced the popular—and allegedly Bolshevist—May 1 holiday. This was the extreme consequence of a fanatical propaganda campaign that asserted that commemorating the birth of Rome was the same as celebrating the birth of the Italian race.

Obviously, the final blow was about to strike Virgil and his works. The Fascist regime couldn't wait to get its hands on the most illustrious and well-known Roman poet in the world, he who had waxed lyrical about the birth of Rome and the advent of the golden age under the leadership of Augustus. In 1924, the Italian (read: Fascist) Society for the Diffusion and Promotion of Classical Studies announced—by way of an article written in Latin that appeared in the magazine *Roma-Atene*—that it would participate in a lavish program of events and publications to commemorate the upcoming anniversary of the birth of Virgil, who in 1930 was about to turn two thousand years old.

For the author of the *Aeneid*, it would be the most inauspicious birthday yet—the flood of *lacrimae rerum* under Fascism was drowning the true meaning of the poem.

* * *

The Fascists didn't organize a celebration of Virgil's bimillennial so much as a circus of horrors and philological errors. In what Luciano Canfora calls "the first mass cultural event with explicit political intentions," all the local chapters of the Fascist Party were encouraged to celebrate the memory of a man that the regime regarded as the prophet of the Italian race. At the same time, a circular from the Ministry was forcing higher education to create a new standardized curriculum that would hold Virgil up as the epic poet of Fascism.

The country saw a flurry of new translations (including one edited by Giuseppe Albini for the Virgil Academy of Mantua and printed in a limited edition of one thousand copies, extravagantly finished), abridged versions for children and parts of the population that had no access to school, university courses, publications and so on.

Plans were drawn up to build a *lucus Virgilii*, a "sacred Virgilian wood," in Virgil's hometown, Pietole, née Andes, a project stewarded by Mussolini's brother Arnaldo. People set to work restoring the tomb of the poet in Naples and the cave of the Sibyl in Cumae. (Apparently under Fascism even the gates of hell needed an upgrade.) The *annus virgilianus* spread to the rest of the world too, with celebrations held in every Italian cultural institute and international classical studies center. One head of such an institute, the painter Albert Besnard, President of the France-Italie Committee and Director of the Académie de France in Rome, saw Virgil as the source of the "fraternal friendship" between the two countries, joined "by a living union of souls" inspired by the poet.

In short, it was all very rhetorical, all very opulent, the whole thing a propaganda operation. And yet it is unclear which Virgil Fascism had in mind. Surely not the Mantuan author of the *Aeneid*, whose life and artistic production were plagued by intellectual doubts and personal crises. Mussolini preferred to imagine Virgil as an old Roman gentleman disdainfully spilling rivers of ink to defend rural Italy and legitimize the empire's mission, a mission that Virgil would naturally have subscribed to and backed unwaveringly; a poet who justified conquering foreign and barbarian lands; a poet so enlightened as to anticipate the Christian origins of his people. All ideas that unfortunately aren't written in the *Eclogues*, the *Georgics* or the *Aeneid*, and don't compute with the poet's biography.

At first it was for his early work's portrayal of country life as industrious and noble that the propaganda wing of the regime tugged—or violently yanked—at Virgil's sleeve. He is mentioned by name, along with uneducated Tityrus in the *Eclogues* and the peasants of the *Georgics*, in the fascist Battle for Grain, a campaign to achieve self-sufficiency in wheat production, as well as in the Pontine Marshes reclamation campaign. Virgil the "country poet" was trotted out on all sorts of occasions to advertise the rural and autarchic model of a new Fascist Italy, which sought to populate the country with small farmers who would be happy to live on little, tirelessly break their backs in the fields, and pummel anybody who questioned their way of life.

We can't help but think of the words from Book 9 quoted earlier, with which Numanus describes the hard education of the first Italic peoples. True, we have to agree with the Fascist academics: that educational model is clearly written in the *Aeneid*. They must have read Virgil's epic at least once. But I doubt they fully absorbed its meaning, seeing as they overlooked the fact that in the *Aeneid* that cave-dwelling and boorish way of life was practiced by the same Italic peoples who meet an ignominious end. Killed or conquered by Aeneas and his foreign ways.

Without the hero from Troy, whose pockets are stuffed not only with household gods but a whole cultural patrimony from the Greek world, the Italy that the Fascists loved to pay lip service to would never have come to be—and the Italic peoples might still be wandering the fields, rake in hand, just the way Mussolini liked it.

* * *

Obviously, georgic and bucolic Virgil didn't suit the regime's propaganda. "The plow cuts the furrow, but the sword defends it," said Mussolini, inaugurating the province of Latina in 1932 (one of the newest provinces, Latina was founded by the Fascists and given the Roman name *Littoria*). Thus the merciless Fascists swung their axe at the *Aeneid* too; unarmed, the epic was dealt a serious blow, and still has the scars to prove it.

We have to hand it to the Fascists, only their onslaught of deceptions could have turned pious Aeneas into a virile and beastly hero, with no blemishes or fears, before whom even Homer's Achilles would have run for the hills. Under the distorted lens of the regime's reading, the hero becomes a fearsome conquistador who does nothing but spill blood on the road to Rome. Fascism would not allow for the anxieties and crippling doubts that are the real hallmarks of Virgilian character, so different from the passionate fury of Homeric heroes.

Suddenly, mild-mannered Aeneas finds himself the strongman advertised by the party as a model citizen under Fascism—the hero goes from *pius* to macho overnight. And modern Italians are meant to look up to this Italian of the past. Never mind that Aeneas was a Trojan who would not pass the regime's purity test. They must also have ignored the condition of the hero as *fato profugos* in Italy, which is clearly stated in line 2, Book 1.

Mussolini went so far as to manipulate the Fates. Fascist imperialism became tinged with grim moral and spiritual—no longer just military and territorial—values. The *Aeneid*, claimed the Fascists, didn't encourage the expansionist and predatory aims of Italy, it dictated them, so that placing pagan and barbarian Africa under the rule of the Roman Empire was part of fate's design (a phrase used by Mussolini in his "proclamation of empire" speech on May 9, 1936).

Not all classicists (though sadly almost all) proved willing to misrepresent the *Aeneid* and its main character as puppets of Fascism. Among those who opposed the regime's propaganda was Tommaso Fiore, who in 1930 published *La Poesia di Virgilio* (Virgil's Poetry), in which he tried to trace the Trojan hero back to the actual text, and in the process caused a stir at the lavish bimillennial ceremonies. More interesting still is how Fascist theorists reacted to critics who tried to bring the reading of Virgil back into the realm of intellectual honesty.

Dissidents were accused of being students of Benedetto Croce and of behaving like academic eggheads, pedantic Latinists in an ivory tower, out of touch with real people (who all of a sudden had a craving for Virgil)—a vexing reaction that is not much different from the one made by people who call anyone possessing an academic title "elitist" or "professorial" in order to table discussions that strive for more than the usual mindless soundbites.

* * *

In this fortress of lies and propaganda, something about the *Aeneid* still jarred with Fascism's glorification of racial purity. Attempts were made to silence and falsify that by no means small detail, but it could not be erased.

It was the mongrel nature of people at the center of the epic—that human and cultural cross-pollination that, according to Virgil, lies at the very foundation of Roman history. Fascist iconography avoided the problem, choosing to skip over Aeneas's Trojan past. Anchises, according to Mussolini's followers, may as well have stayed behind to die in Troy and not weighed on the backs, and futures, of others. It is interesting to note how the most symbolic scene in the *Aeneid*, when the father is borne on his son's shoulders, a scene that has been depicted time and again, is comfortably left out of official Fascist art. The Fascists preferred to think of Aeneas in the role of brave solitary captain, one that has no basis in the text.

Yet the verses written by Virgil are crystal clear—you cannot just tear out the pages of the *Aeneid* that don't suit your narrative. In Book 12, just as the epic is about to conclude, we read:

If victory is ours, as I believe it will be,
and the powers of the gods confirm as much,
I'll not demand that Latins bow to Trojans
nor ask that I be king. Two undefeated peoples
shall share equal laws by an eternal pact.
(12.187-191)

This is Aeneas speaking. He addresses Juno directly, promising to treat the defeated as equals and not impose on them Trojan laws and traditions. Instead, they will live as one people, united. Forgive my candor, but Aeneas did us a big favor by sparing the people of Latium from becoming the latest link in the chain of ignorant, subjugated, and enslaved generations.

In every story there are winners and there are losers. In the *Aeneid*, the losers are the same Italic peoples lionized by Fascism as pioneers of Italian character—when in fact their crude customs and violent ways will be immediately snuffed out. Aeneas wins, and with him the traditions of the Greeks: Their diverse culture will live on and be bequeathed to us.

It always eluded the Fascist regime that the one reason Italy and its values exist is because the Latins and the Trojans made a multiethnic, multicultural pact that gave rise to a new, mixed people: the Romans. That's where we come from. Not elsewhere. Were I to put this hybrid vision of the world as described by the *Aeneid* in mathematical terms, it might look something like this:

Trojan + Italic People = Romans (and later Italians and Europeans)

So why does Italy not bear the name of its Trojan victors? Why do we not speak Greek? Virgil is quick to respond: Because farsighted Zeus wills it so. Finally forced to swallow the defeat of his protected peoples, the father of the gods will accept Juno's request:

I ask one thing which fate does not deny,
for Latium's sake and for the honor of your own:
Once they have brokered peace by marriage (let them
be happy!), once they've established laws and pacts,
let the native Latins keep their ancient name.
Do not make them answer to the name Trojans
or Teucrians, or change their tongue or dress.
Let Latium stand, let Alban kings reign for ages.
Empower the Roman line with Italian virtue.
Troy fell. Its name should fall with it.
(12.819-828)

Troy fell, and Rome was born. The terms established

by the gods, that the people who to this day inhabit Italy are part of a melting pot, are crystal clear. Also clear is the divine command that the marriage between the peoples *felicibus esto*—be happy.

Now that we've debunked the Fascists' groundless interpretations, Aeneas can return to these parts, bearing the burden of the past on his shoulders and holding the unknown future by the hand.

8
MIRABILE DICTU:
STYLE AND HEXAMETERS IN THE *AENEID*

In me you morph
into a music of countless keys
and voices and cries.
Water, wind, silence—
music pours out of you!
And my hostile
obscurity grows troubled,
my blood boils
with this aching anxiety
for the open harpsichord,
to have a purpose,
to be, like you,
music; and become,
in you, for you,
water, silence, wind,
a clear melody
against the meaningless, bitter
cry in the dark.
—GIORGIO MANGANELLI, "Three Movements for Harpsichord,
III," in *Poems*

A concerto might be the most fitting metaphor to
describe Virgil's poetic style. That would explain the

reactions of readers throughout history who, encountering the hexameters of the *Aeneid*, immediately pine for Homer and complain they're bored. They thought they had tickets to a heavy metal show and instead found themselves seated before a philharmonic.

At the opposite end of the style spectrum is Homer: the rock star, obviously. The *Aeneid* doesn't invent a language that astonishes for its power and beauty, like that of Homer, whose voice is the only one to emerge from the silence of the distant past, like Venus born out of the blue sea. But that doesn't mean that Virgil's Latin is cold or detached, or that the poet employs the pedantic language of a bureaucrat.

Sure, the *Aeneid* is not incandescent, hot-to-the-touch material. It is not cut from the same cloth with which the *Iliad* and *Odyssey* are woven. Virgil's epic is more like a symphony; the linguistic spectacle that he creates captivates for its grace, not for its furor; it does not explore the unknown but enlarges the known, with the limpidity of certain ocean floors or certain eyes—his clarity is always tinged with melancholy. Paul Veyne claims that Virgil is "the ancient poet most like Mozart." I would go a step further. Reading the *Aeneid* produces in us the same inner restiveness as listening to Mozart's symphony No. 40 in G minor, K. 550, when performed, say, by Arturo Toscanini's orchestra. Not the unbridled joy of euphoria, but the steady joy of the andante, slowly gathering steam, never resorting to loud wails.

Virgil's Language

To describe Virgil's style by way of a literary analogy instead of a musical one: Imagine the effect of opening up the stories of Anton Chekhov or Raymond Carver for the first time, right after having read *One Hundred Years of Solitude* by Gabriel García Márquez. Like Colonel Buendía at the start of the Columbian Nobel laureate's novel, Homer confronted a world without the words to express the social phenomena of ancient Greece. The poet furnished them himself, with neologisms, prefixes and suffixes, and a highly personal use of verb tenses and grammatical aspects, features that would combine to create what we call to this day Homeric Greek.

On the other hand, the world that Virgil was compelled to depict was, alas, visible to every Roman citizen, who anxiously tried to make sense of what was happening in the centuries-old history of the S.P.Q.R. There was no shortage of words, a literary tradition had already been firmly established. Moreover, the powers that be were demanding torrents of words, Augustus first and foremost; the emperor expected the *Aeneid* to immortalize the fulfillment of Rome's destiny in verse.

Virgil had the opposite problem of Homer: All too many words had been spent, and all too many had been manipulated. It was an arduous task to select those words that had managed to evade the fleeting prose of the official narrative and earn the name poetry. There was neither the time nor the space for blurring lines. "Now is not the time for spectacles," the Sibyl says to Aeneas just before they descend to the Underworld, as the hero stands mesmerized by the sophisticated artwork adorning the doors of the Temple of Apollo in Cumae (6.37).

In the *Aeneid*, Virgil pursues greatness via restraint. Affect is prohibited, rhetorical flourishes forbidden, big explosions banned. His verse is vigorous not because it is cold but because it insists on balance—like someone in troubled waters calling for calm. The poet rejects the shabbier register of prose yet never pushes his poetry beyond the limits of elegance and clarity. Next to him, even the widely celebrated Ovid sounds turgid and redundant. There is no room for the triumphant declamation that the emperor so wanted, yet every verse rings lyrical.

There are very few neologisms for the sake of neologisms, fashioned purely to shock the reader; almost all are archaisms or Greek-isms or poeticisms fished from common speech. At this point there is little to invent, though many twists remain to be understood. It is impossible to find a superfluous word in the epic. Even when the narrative emotes, elegance is not abandoned. If there is a feeling to express, Virgil expresses it in a few words, without wildly gesticulating.

Whether the story of Aeneas's vicissitudes is communicating terror or compassion, ardor or sadness, tenderness or, on the rare occasion, wit, it conveys it through the personal language of Virgil—*within* his style, never without. The poet has dramatic empathy for all the characters in the epic but never allows himself to make a point of his sympathies or antipathies.

True, pathos might be missing from the *Aeneid*, or

at least that visceral emotional transport of Homer that makes us cry with Hector and Achilles. The point is that Virgil doesn't care about pleasure—not the reader's pleasure as much as the pleasure of those to whom the *Aeneid* was addressed. Maybe Virgil didn't like the feeling himself. Who can say? Surely the poet doesn't want us—doesn't expect us—to sob over the fates of Aeneas and Anchises.

If there are tears left to be shed, owing to the style of the *Aeneid*, we shed them for ourselves alone. To borrow Virgil's words, *spes sibi quisque*—everyone finds hope from within (11.309).

The Question of Style

The *Aeneid* does not have a Phemius or Demodocus, the bards in the *Odyssey* who sing at the courts of Alcinous and Penelope, introducing readers to the very first metaliterary scene and igniting arguments over the role of poetry that, after three millennia, have yet to be resolved.

However, there is a singular character in Book 9, Drances, "silver tongued, but in times of war slack armed." Through Drances's provocations and the answers of his interlocutor, Turnus, we can glean the substance of Virgil's verse style, beginning with the refinement he picked up in his youth at the Roman schools of rhetoric. Drances is an old courtier who weaves plots at the court of King Latinus. A weak chief but an excellent politician and orator, after a lengthy panegyric about Aeneas and the Trojans, Drances

makes an elaborate speech to the sovereign, who is petrified at the prospect of Latium's likely defeat. The speech
is underhanded, since Drances's true aim is to discredit
Turnus (toward whom he bears a personal grudge) and see
him die in battle.

For the first time in this epic poem held together by
stylistic poise and verbal accuracy that border on the
divine, Virgil permits himself a piece of bravura in this
ars oratoria, which he himself had promptly abandoned
to dedicate himself entirely to poetry. The first part of
Drances' speech relies on a rhetorical topos, the *recusa-
tio*, a refusal to touch on a subject that is already well
known *urbi et orbi*, i.e., to Rome and the world. But his
demurral has hints of populism: There is no need to rely
on hard words or lofty arguments outside the common
tongue, because by now everybody knows that the kingdom has been put in jeopardy by the obstinacy of Turnus
to move against Aeneas.

Drances proceeds to urge Latinus to rethink his position
and marry his daughter Lavinia to the Trojan hero, a hero
he paints as so powerful that, if Troy had had two men like
Aeneas, it would still be standing and "Greece would be the
one weeping" (11.287). Their only guarantee of "peace with
a lasting pact" is to join the Trojans, continues the courtier,
and not be simply thrown together, as the king, in extremis,
has earlier proposed, even considering out loud whether to
offer parcels of land to the Trojans so that they could settle
in Latium but remain separate from the Latins.

He concludes his speech with an anguished and slightly
melodramatic plea that Latinus waste no time evacuating

the battlefield and that Turnus offer himself up to Aeneas posthaste. Drances sues for peace, but what he really wants is for his rival to fall on Aeneas's sword. He uses a very effective turn of phrase to implore Turnus to at least show his fellow citizens respect, since it is on account of his persistent barbarity that they risk falling like *animae viles, inhumate infletaque turba*, "base animals, unburied and unwept" (11.372)—"cannon fodder," in the parlance of the nineteenth century; "meat for slaughter" today.

Turnus breathes. He listens patiently and does not lose his cool. His response—equally assiduous though in a style that stands in stark contrast to Draces's—may contain Virgil's own response to critics who would accuse the *Aeneid* of lacking pathos. Here (11.378-82) is the king of the Rutulians replying to the fussy courtesan:

> "You, Drances, never want for words
> when what the war requires is arms. Counsellors
> call a meeting, and you get there first. You fill
> the halls with soaring words from your safe perch
> while the enemies are just outside the walls
> and the trenches are about to fill with blood."

Right. Easy to be a "counsellor," teacher, critic, and editor of other people's style from a safe perch, so Virgil seems to be saying, while "the enemies are just outside the walls." Simple, perhaps even justifiable, to make demands with "soaring words" in times of peace. It's impossible not to think of the famous "winged words" (*epea pteroenta*) that appear over 120 times (!) in the *Iliad* and *Odyssey*. But when the trenches are flowing with blood, the war requires more than pandering; it demands "arms," and a few carefully chosen words.

At the time that Virgil was writing the *Aeneid*, all the defenses of the Roman Republic, including its verbal defenses, had fallen, and the trench separating it from dictatorship was filled with dead bodies and empty speeches. Among the ruins lay the former grandeur of Latin poetry, with its model epicists, Ennius and Naevius (we'll get to them in a minute), who had the nerve to prematurely set down in verse the birth of Rome. Virgil had a pressing need to come up with a new style for the *Aeneid*; rhetorical flourishes were no longer viable in his day, neither for looking back at the past nor for imagining the future.

Those are the reasons behind a style that makes order its cardinal rule and organic unity the linchpin around which the plot is structured. Virgil either cannot or does not want to natter and drift or display his personal virtuosity as he describes the actions of Aeneas. When he does feel compelled to take a position, he does so stealthily, without resorting to a glut of words (usually a handful will do), proving he is an old master of "show don't tell." Because the equilibrium that Virgil seeks in his verses is the same that is desperately needed by an entire generation that has no more energy for the exuberant poetry of Plautus or the opulent verbiage of Cicero.

Virgil's hexameters are not the only things trying to keep their balance while enemy troops advance. It was the age, brought to its knees, that wanted to make determination and restraint the style of perseverance.

* * *

O, honor and light of other poets,
avail me the long study and great love
that made me search your volume.

You are my master and author, you
alone are the one from whom I took
the noble style that brought me honor.
(DANTE, *Inferno*, 1.82-87)

The time has come to examine more closely the "noble style" of the *Aeneid* to which Dante, in the opening of his *Commedia*, professes his debt, because of which he chooses Virgil, "honor and light" of all poets, to guide him through the Underworld. Obviously, the *Aeneid* draws on the Latin of lofty poetry, a language vastly different from the prose of Cicero or Cornelius Nepos. Here, *arms* means war, not weapons; *arena* means dust, not sand; *tempora* stands for forehead, not temples; *vir* often replaces the pronoun *is* (he) and does not necessarily mean man. The use of simple verb forms in place of compound verb forms was common in Latin poetry, which had to adapt to the strict alternation of long and short syllables imposed by the meter.

But Virgil uses the device because he takes pleasure in its elegance; he doesn't overly worry about the meter, which he seems to have a handle on just fine. So in the *Aeneid* we find *venire* rather than *advenire* (to arrive); *piare* rather than *expiare* (to expiate/atone); *solari* and not *consolari* (to comfort); *servare* and not *observare* (to observe). Neuter plural nouns are extremely frequent, which is to say that neuter plural nouns retain their singular meaning: Troy is always referred to as *regna*, not *regnum*; *templa* (temples) have *tecta* (roofs), even if the temple being talked about clearly has just one *tectum*; and the gods never drink *vinum* (wine), only *vina* (wines).

A distinguishing feature of Virgil's poetry is its frequent reliance on hysteron proteron—from the Greek ὕστερον πρότερον, ὕστερον (later) and πρότερον (earlier)—a rhetorical device in which the chronology of two ideas is inverted in order to emphasize the first. One legendary hysteron proteron, cited as an example of the device in many Italian textbooks, is found in line 353 of Book 2: *moriamur et in media arma ruamus*—Let us die and charge into battle. Equally well known is a hysteron proteron combined with an example of hypallage in line 268 of Book 6: *ibant obscuri sola sub noctem per umbram*—on into the dark they went, alone in the night, through the shadows.

Even more interesting are the stylistic affects that can be attributed to no one else but Virgil and will make his Latin the official language of all poetry to come after him and his *Aeneid* the schoolbook for dozens of generations, from the Roman Empire through the Middle Ages and the Renaissance and finally on up to us and our children. When he wants to render a ceremony more solemn, Virgil employs a bold sequence typical of the oratory style of lawyers—he does not give in to the banal enumerations of prose. Here are some verses, lines 666 and 667 in Book 9, that stand on the shoulders of a three-part parallel sequence known as *tricola,* or tricolon—from Greek *tri* (three) and *kolon* (member)—which create a cadenced, Martial-like movement: "the ground is strewn with arrows, shields and hollow helmets / rattle as they're struck, the bitter battle swells."

There are instances of bold synesthesia in the *Aeneid*, which would enchant the likes of Charles Baudelaire and Victor Hugo many centuries later. Hugo actually began his career as a poet translating the verses of Virgil, whom he called his *maître divin,* divine master, as he addresses him in the poem "À *Virgile*" in *Les voix intérieures,* 1837. In line 588, Book 12, for example, smoke is first described as "bitter" and then its odor becomes "black," creating a poetic blur of taste, smell, and color.

If, in analyzing the dramaturgy of Virgil, we rightly make reference to the *Iliad* and *Odyssey*, we must also allow that the *Aeneid* makes a nearly infinite number of stylistic allusions to other Greek and Latin authors. It would be impossible to name them all here, given the depth of Virgil's reading and poetic sensibility, which leads him to engage even minor writers completely lost to us today. We would be justified in scouring the *Aeneid* for traces of his friend Cornelius Gallus—if only we had more to go on than his naked name.

There isn't an ancient writer who eludes Virgil, nor is there a stylistic effect not called into service in the poem. Among his favorite allusions mention should be made of Apollonius of Rhodes and the elegant alexandrines of his *Argonautica*; Catullus and his shocking love poems; and his contemporaries Ovid and Propertius. But there are also references to Plato's philosophy and even to the Epicurean rigor of Lucretius, whose *De rerum natura* the poet seems to be in conversation with in more than one passage in the *Aeneid*.

* * *

Miserabile visu—"Miserable to see" (1.111)
Horresco referens—"Horrible to repeat" (2.204)
Mirabile dictu—"Marvelous to tell" (1.439)

The *Aeneid* is full of the above expressions, significant for their use of the rare ablative of the supine construction. In the Latin text of the epic that I used when putting together this book, Gian Biagio Conte puts them in parentheses. They are instances of Virgil speaking directly to the reader and revealing what he feels and remembers as he tells his story.

Critics have, for some time now, taken to talking about how modern the *Aeneid* is, its subjective style—a definition canonized by the American Brooks Otis in the 1960s—making Virgil's epic a contemporary novel, distinct from the rigidity that characterizes the works of Homer. However, that does not mean that Virgil takes the liberty of intruding on the *Aeneid* whenever he feels like commenting on the progress of the narrative.

As I have said repeatedly, the poet is very careful about shielding his readers from having to sift through personal and autobiographical details of no concern to them. Virgil has absolutely nothing to say about himself, much less something to teach us. His epic is not a heartbreaking memoir nor a didactic essay. The extraordinary modernity of the *Aeneid* and its subjective style—next to which the

Iliad and the *Odyssey* seem almost archaic, fossilized in the impersonal and objective grandeur with which their author narrates them—does not lie in some moral pact or ethical position taken by the poet. After all, like his readers, Virgil cannot boast of having seen his city fall after a decade-long siege in the greatest war the ancient world had ever known. Nor of having sailed the seas, loved an African queen, or founded a kingdom destined for unimaginable greatness.

Simply put, Virgil is human. He inhabits the same ephemeral dimension as everyone else. More importantly, he writes from that dimension. All the poet is saying with his brief interjections is, I know how it feels. I shudder at the thought of grief. I love remembering my mother. I still can't get over that betrayal. When he watches his characters triumph or die, he recognizes the scent of happiness and the whiff of defeat. That is all—it is not to be taken for granted and it is not insignificant. It is not an affectation either: If the poet's words quoted above seem plain, that is the result not of false modesty but of his desperate need to level with us.

That is exactly where Virgil's modernity is to be found, in the sincerity with which he chose the *Aeneid*'s point of view. That is what makes his style so *mirabile dictu*— wonderful to relate. And wonderful to remember, too; as anyone who has read the *Aeneid* in Latin can tell you, these brief, almost formulaic phrases are often the hardest to forget.

The Question of the Hexameter

Timeo Danaos et dona ferentis, I fear the Greeks even when they bear gifts (2.49).

Thus Laocoon warns the Trojans about the wooden horse that the Greeks leave at the gates of Troy. In spite of his warning, Latin poetry would eagerly welcome a present from Greece without which there would be no *Aeneid*. Or at least not in the glorious form we read it today. That Greek gift is the meter in which Virgil wrote the epic. The hexameter had been the standard meter of epic poetry since Homer's day. In Italian schools, we learn to recognize it in Latin, and—with a lot of sweat and tears—how to scan it by studying the verses of the *Aeneid*.

Now is a good time to briefly go over the structure, for those not fortunate enough to have the rhythm of classical meter in their blood. Dactylic hexameter, more commonly known as hexameter as far back as Herodotus, is a metrical line consisting of six dactyls—the term comes from the Greek *hex*, or six, and *metron*, or measure, foot. Each line has one long syllable followed by either another long syllable or two short syllables, with the final foot composed of two syllables, the first long and the second either long or short. The meter can be written out like so:

$$- \overset{\smile}{\smile} \mid -\overset{\smile}{\smile} \mid -\overset{\smile}{\smile} \mid -\overset{\smile}{\smile} \mid -\smile\smile \mid -\text{X}$$

For those of us—myself included—who begin hyperventilating at the sight of these weird symbols, recalling hours at our desks scratching crooked marks into our copies of the *Aeneid*, and now can't read a single verse without hiccupping through the syllables like a broken record, it would behoove us to recall that, however ancient Latin was really pronounced, the ancient poets no doubt recited hexameters with naturalness and ease.

More generally, dactylic hexameter was the rhythm employed when reading aloud or reciting, a harmonious cadence with imperceptible pauses between one word and another. The meter undergirded the music of the Latin, whether prose or poetry; it was a melody that permeated the entire text and which Romance languages have almost completely lost, since they are endowed with qualitative, not quantitative, rhythms, and therefore make no distinction between long and short syllables.

To return to academic scars, the recitation of Latin hexameter verse was most certainly sinuous and graceful, not punctuated by long pauses or interrupted by nervous hemming and hawing. Nowadays there is an astonishing amount of imaginative resources for learning how to read Latin hexameter verse: audio files, interactive learning tools, and tutorial videos prove that technologies come and go, but the nightmare inflicted on us by classical meter remains unchanged.

We have to admit, getting back to ancient Rome, that the introduction of the hexameter freed Latin verse from its primitive and raw form. Because the first Roman to answer the call of the Muse and compose verse, whoever it may have been, adopted another meter: Saturnian verse. This home-grown verse was named after Saturn, who, as we have seen in the chapter on the Italic peoples in the *Aeneid*, chose to

take refuge in Latium after he was deposed by Jupiter. Other
sources refer to the meter as Faunian, after the god Faunus,
an ancient creature with a human body but the hoofs and
horns of a goat, another descendent of Saturn, venerated in
remote times during the Lupercalia, ceremonies with music
and dance to protect flocks and herds from being attacked by
wolves (Lupercus was another name for Faunus).

Without getting into the difficult and ill-defined structure of the Saturnian (which may have been composed
of a catalectic iambic dimeter and an ithyphallic or by a
'versus reizianus' separated by a diaeresis, or short natural
break), there are only two things that we can say for certain
about this Latin meter. First, that the Romans had a poetic
tradition that preceded the influence of Greek culture as
attested to by numerous ancient ritual phrases. Second, that
no one cared for this unrefined Roman proto-literature, not
even the Romans, who rushed to embrace the Trojan horse
of Homeric poetry and its elegant hexameters.

Everyone knows Horace's famous line, *Graecia capta
ferum victorem cepit*. Greece, the captive, made her savage
victor captive. Few know that it refers to the Greek verse that
would substitute ancient Latin meter which the poet did not
hesitate to call *horridus*—literally horrid. The exact words in
the *Epistles* with which Horace celebrates the advent of the
hexameter in Rome, to the detriment of the rustic Saturnian,
are these: "Captive Greece made her savage [Roman] victor
captive and brought the arts into agrarian Latin lands. Thus
the rude Saturnian measure faded and taste expelled the
rank poison" (*Epistles*, 2.1.156-159).

* * *

If, as tradition has it, Rome was founded by Romulus in 753 BC, Roman literature would have to wait over five hundred years for someone to dare set down its first verse. That wait was somehow made up for by the spectacularity—and extravagance, when compared with the seriousness of Hesiod's *Theogony*—with which Roman poetry was born. Historians credit Livius Andronicus with launching Latin poetry. A freed slave of Greek origin, born in Taranto, Italy, around 284 BC, Livius made a name for himself in Rome as a dramatist, actor, mime, and, during the Second Punic War, the author of almost mystical intercessory hymns.

Though only a few fragments of Livius's work survive, we can safely say he didn't lack for ambition, knowing that, driven by a desire to introduce the Greek myths to Rome, Livius set to work translating the *Odyssey* into Latin and adopted the Saturnian to do so. His theatrical adaptation of Homer's epic, the *Odyssia*, brought Latin literature to light in 240 BC. It must have cost Livius a great effort to carry over into Latin the syntax and lexical richness of the Greek language and dare to adapt the social customs, religious ceremonies, and names of the Greek gods for a Roman public. To say nothing of the hexameter, which Andronicus transformed, one line at a time, into homespun Saturnians.

Forty fragments are all that is left of the *Odyssia*. Despite Cicero's excoriation of the work—in *Brutus* he derides the epic as not worth a second read—readers can judge for themselves with what dexterity Livius turned the first verse of Homer's Odyssey into Latin:

Virum mihi, Camena, insece versutum.
Sing to me, Camena, of the cunning hero.

The German historian Barthold Georg Niebuhr went so far as to brand Roman poetry "dead on arrival" for its reliance, from the outset, on Greek forms and stories, but evaluations of originality aside, as far as this book is concerned, what matters is that Virgil was not the first to set his sights on where it all began, i.e., on the fall of Troy. Instead, the *Aeneid* explicitly aims to represent the apotheosis of the Roman poetic tradition, which had always sought perfection and dignity by expressly and unembarrassedly making reference to the Greek tradition. Moreover, Virgil must have read and studied Livius's *Odyssia*. Unfortunately, it is now impossible to determine whether there are references to the earlier epic in the *Aeneid*.

Bearing in mind the current approach to teaching the classics, it is curious to note that the first Latin poet found the pluck—the audacity—to take on such a monumental task not by order of a politician or Muse but because his students asked him to. Apparently, the idea of translating Homer's *Odyssey* and adapting it for Roman audiences came to Livius while he was discharging his duties as a *grammaticus*, which is to say, while he was teaching Greek and Latin to children from patrician families, families who saw literature as fundamental to the education of Rome's future ruling class. From that point on, until at least the first century BC, the *Odyssia* became the textbook with which every Roman boy tackled the Greek language. Horace's recollection, in Book 2 of the *Epistles*, of studying Greek to the beat of his teacher's rod is unforgettable (and timeless).

Nevertheless, in the early years of the Roman Empire, Livius's poetic labors would be blanked over—and his *Odyssia* binned. For centuries, another schoolbook would occupy its spot on every child's desk, and this time the text was not Greek but proudly Latin. It was Virgil's *Aeneid*.

* * *

Once Livius had paved the way for Homeric-inspired Roman poetry, there were still two more legs of the journey before Virgil could give free rein to his resourcefulness. The first leg—the narration in verse of Aeneas's escape from Troy and flight to Latium—had been completed by an impetuous Campanian poet named Gnaeus Naevius. Of Oscan origin, an authority on Greek and Siceliot culture, Naevius became better known for his irreverent and satirical verve than for his aspirations as a tragedian; for slandering the Metelli family and Scipio Africanus, he was imprisoned and later died an exile in Utica, around 201 BC.

Naevius devoted his last years to writing the *Bellum Poenicum*, an epic poem in Saturnian meter that narrates the history of Rome, from its founding by Aeneas to the First Punic War, in which Naevius himself had fought. It is difficult to judge the style of the poem, the first epic primarily about Rome, since all that remain of it are sixty odd fragments, few more than three lines long. As for the story, in which Aeneas sojourns in Dido's Carthage, there is no doubt that Virgil took cues from it to sketch out the plot of his *Aeneid*.

With Aeneas placed on the poetic route that led from Troy to Rome, all that the Latin epic needed not to do was shuffle off the crude Saturnian meter. Enter Quintus Ennius, a poet born in Rudiae (near Lecce, Italy) in 239 BC and endowed, as he put it (and as Aulus Gellius recorded in *Attic Nights*), with "three hearts," *tria cordia*, one of the most beautiful metaphors to describe the languages which he spoke and in which he wrote: Oscan, Latin, and Greek. With his exhaustive knowledge of literature and serious, determined temperament—he lived on his writing and died impoverished—Ennius dedicated much of his life to writing the *Annals*, a sweeping history of Rome narrated year by year, from its origins to the year 171 BC, shortly before his death.

Since ancient times, Ennius has been acknowledged as the father of Latin poetry for his revolutionary use of Greek hexameters instead of the Latin Saturnian, a decision he proudly undertook in the *Annals*. Of the eighteen books that make up his epic, there remain roughly six thousand fragments, including the proem, in which Ennius claims to be the reincarnation of Homer, via the transmigration of souls, and that Homer is now compelling him to produce poetry worthy of the name for the history of Roman literature. For over a century, the *Annals* of Ennius—whom Horace dubbed *alter Homerus*, "the other Homer"—was Rome's major national poem. It was impossible for a writer not to look to it as a model; it was disqualifying for a politician not to publicly declare his love for it.

In fact, the somber style of the *Annals*, restrained and still a bit bumpy—especially given the stiff (largely spondaic) hexameters—and admired by the fiercest defenders of *romanitas*, like Cato the Elder, became the emblem of the Roman Republic. Ennius's *Annals* was the great collective story of the Republican era, which, to the beat of scowling hexameters, was described as an age of stable institutions, populated by serious and responsible *cives* whose sole ambition was to honor the moral legacy of their founding fathers.

So, when first Caesar and then Augustus decided they had had enough of all that and that the time had come to establish an empire, poetry remained speechless—and the *Annals* turned out to be wholly inadequate, and anachronistic. Ennius's three hearts were not up to the task of narrating the age of emperors.

Two and half centuries after Livius's *Odyssia*, Virgil had all that he needed to write the *Aeneid*. By the time he came along, Greek mythology had been completely assimilated into Roman culture and the dignified hexameter was the official meter of Latin poetry. But Virgil had a subtle advantage over his predecessors: his own elegance, a gift unique to him, not tied to any model, which would lead to the creation of incomparable verses for the very reason that Virgil did not feel as though he was being compared to anyone. Imperial poetry had shaken off the inferiority complex that had plagued Ennius's age: Rome was no longer indebted to Greek literature, and no one would be so publicly barbarous as to criticize the use of Hellenic models, as they had back in the unsophisticated Republican era.

Virgil wasn't asked to measure up to Homer; he was asked to surpass him.

So, ever since the posthumous publication of the *Aeneid* in 19 BC, Latin poetry has had just one stylistic model, which has been imitated countless times over the course of centuries: Virgil's style.

FORTUNE FAVORS THE BOLD:
THE LITERARY RECEPTION OF THE *AENEID*

O you departing
with a heavy suitcase
and two green eyes,
with Simone Weil
and two hard breasts;
take note, and don't forget,
that on this unlikely planet
one man alone
can properly pronounce your name.
—GIORGIO MANGANELLI, from *Poems*

To begin talking about what happened to the *Aeneid* after its publication, we must enlist the aid of the German language, with its precise, untranslatable words for expressing the most powerful abstractions that human thought is capable of. In this case, the apt word is *Nachleben*, or "afterlife, survival." As applied in art criticism, the word owes its existence to Aby Warburg, who argued that the presence of classical forms in the collective imagination is so pervasive as to transcend individual poetic style and the interpretation of a single work of art.

On the other hand, turning our attention to the wild

fortunes of Virgil's epic over the centuries, to the hundreds of spin-offs and imitators, to the uninterrupted academic study of the text, to its manifestation in every poetic language that demands dignity, those of us limited to the vagaries of Neo-Latin languages would no doubt say that the *Aeneid* has had "*fortuna*," success. Frankly, it's been a "triumph."

But that's not exactly how things stand—and "success" may not be the right word.

An Ancient Present

Despite the history of critical praise of the *Aeneid*, the text has long been met with a certain kind of snobbery, with readers who turn their nose up at the epic for being a byproduct of Augustan propaganda or a forgery of Greek tales—two misconceptions that my own book has already debunked. At times Virgil has been treated like a politician who wins an election without anyone having apparently voted for him: endlessly circulated, copied out at will, yet no clear arguments on behalf of the beauty of the *Aeneid*. During other periods in history, especially the most tumultuous, Virgil has been regarded as a saint, a miracle worker, a prophet capable of healing present woes, and amid the panic of the moment, all literary precision is jettisoned.

So, what exactly has happened since 19 BC, when Emperor Augustus published the epic against the author's will? It's a fascinating story, for the *Aeneid* survived mostly by surviving itself.

Our inquiry immediately presents us with a strange paradox. There is every reason to label the *Aeneid*, in marketing jargon, a "literary sensation," a "hands-down bestseller." Virgil vies with Homer for first place in the canon of secular Western literature, and even comes close to overtaking the Greek bard, since for almost five hundred years, during the Middle Ages, Europeans lost the ability to read Greek, and the *Aeneid* became the Latin textbook for every student in an education system that had long foregrounded the study of rhetoric.

From a philological perspective, it's surprising to discover that, in terms of the quantity and quality of illuminated manuscripts of his work, Virgil is the only author to come close to the Old Testament. Two manuscripts merit special mention: The *Vergilius Vaticanus* and the *Vergilius Romanus*. Written in rustic capitals in the fifth century, both manuscripts are magnificently illustrated—and are the oldest illuminated manuscripts in the history of non-Christian codicology, along with the *Ilias picta* (here, too, Virgil beats Homer, two codices to one). Based on the number of reproductions and commentaries, panegyrics and epigones, paraphrases and translations of the *Aeneid* that have proceeded apace for two thousand years, we might expect Virgil to be our collective hero, the symbol of literature in Italy and all of Europe, with Greece the sole exception.

In light of the epic's plaudits, you'd think that children from Augustus's day to our own have gone to bed listening to the story of brave Aeneas, have been eager to dress as the exiled Trojan for Halloween, have begged for an illustrated copy of the *Aeneid* for their birthday. You would think that

Virgil would be the patron saint of the city of Rome and that the city would be full of large-scale monuments and altars strewn with fragrant flowers in honor of his work. Let me inform readers who don't know any better—lest they become, by the end of this essay, innocent tourists, like Ingrid Bergman in Roberto Rossellini's *Viaggio in Italia*—that to my knowledge no one has the *Aeneid* by heart or recites it in the public square, not in Rome, not in Mantua, not anywhere in the Bel Paese.

As I've said elsewhere, I have never seen anyone's chest swell at the sound of Aeneas's name. Nor have I ever felt particularly proud about the fact Virgil and I hail from the same country, and it has never occurred to me to flaunt it when abroad. And yet, in light of what looks like collective amnesia, the *Aeneid* has never been lost in the annals of history or consigned to the same dustbin into which even very good works of art fall, time having gotten the better of them, so that they no longer speak to our present moment. As he was yesterday and as he will probably be tomorrow (we hope), Virgil is still actively taught at school, whole chapters of Italian and Latin textbooks and anthologies are dedicated to him, every so often a book about the myth of Aeneas or a film about the founding of Rome is released, and art exhibits are frequently devoted to his image. To say nothing of all the times that the *Aeneid* is trotted out by politicians, almost invariably apropos of nothing, to justify racist or purist claims, or, vice-versa, to remind us of the basic duty to welcome those who cross the sea to Italy, defeated and seeking refuge, just like Aeneas.

Hated and beatified, rejected and endlessly imitated,

Virgil and the *Aeneid* have taken a winding path toward literary permanence, one that eludes simple chronology—chronology understood as a succession of individual moments. There's no point in flipping through literary anthologies and trying to trace, chapter by chapter, some form of magical influence that Virgil had on later authors: You wouldn't find much, because the *Aeneid* doesn't provide readers with a set of myths that can go on being expanded ad infinitum, unlike the *Iliad* and *Odyssey*, which, after three thousand years, we still have not stopped probing and—especially—rewriting. The *Aeneid*, on the other hand, has given us a means to orient ourselves when we arrive at the kind of major crossroads that humanity has encountered over the course of history—a means of looking chaos in the face and putting the pieces back together as best we can. It is not, therefore, a matter of a constant or diachronic presence—author after musician after sculptor reading Virgil and passing him down through the centuries. It's a matter of the *Aeneid*'s "survival," i.e., *Nachleben*. The epic has fallen silent during times of peace and prosperity, when it has had nothing to say, only to answer the call every time events have driven us to consult it.

For centuries Virgil's epic was silenced or regarded as off-key, critiqued, with unjustified hubris, as inferior to Homer, only for it to become indispensable again in times of crisis, when people would take to praying to the *Aeneid* as if it were a miraculous book. What's more, in the history of literature the *Aeneid* has never belonged to the past, but, from the start, to the present, in that hall of mirrors in which Aeneas's future was becoming Rome's past—a constant present, yes, yet always ancient too, capable of foretelling the age to come by looking to the past.

Aeneid *Mania: Paganism, Christianity, Alchemy*

In line 284 of Book 10, we read: *Audentis Fortuna iuvat*, "fortune favors the bold." The phrase immediately became an immortal motivational mantra for when the going gets tough.

Far be it from me to say whether or not Virgil was a brave man (though personally I think he was). But it is beyond dispute that, as he wrote the epic, he lacked neither for lucidity nor self-control. Long before the *Aeneid* was published, the epic was highly anticipated, the talk of Rome.

Once Virgil accepted Augustus's charge, the nascent empire set its sights on him for at least a decade. While the poet was busy writing, and, to concentrate, moving farther and farther away from the Caput Mundi (first Naples, then his long trip to Greece), literary circles began arguing over the *Aeneid*—presumably without having read more than a few lines of it. Virgil's epic was quickly met with debates, reviews, raves, and pans written by a small number of hard-to-please intellectuals who were embittered by the attacks on free speech taking place under Augustus's Principate—and by their inability to find words with more teeth in them than empty flattery.

Apparently, Virgil was neither prey to performance anxiety nor especially prone to stress, since he managed to endure the (hardly sober) way his friends and fellow poets in Augustan circles took to trumpeting the supremacy of the *Aeneid* before it was finished. Of all the enthusiastic praise, none tops Propertius, who writes of Virgil's work: "Make way, Roman authors! Make way, you Greeks! Something greater than the *Iliad* is about to be born!" The Mantuan poet must have kept a cool head; anyone else would have given up writing altogether the moment his book was compared favorably to Homer.

Of the fierce prepublication debates among detractors and supporters, nothing but faint echoes are left. And confirmation that, long before its publication, all of Rome was wondering the same thing we have been wondering for two thousand years: Is the *Aeneid* really *the* epic Roman poem, inspired by Greek models but so brilliant as to surpass them?

When Virgil died and Augustus, with the help of Virgil's friends Plotius Tucca and Varius Rufus, published the epic, there erupted an *Aeneid* mania in Rome, a mania that would last a long time. Explicit reference to Virgil was made by every single writer of the next generation. Authors of all genres quoted the *Aeneid*: the philosopher Seneca, the naturalist Pliny the Elder, the poet Martial, and the historian Tacitus. And, to prove the old saying that truth is stranger than fiction, apparently Nero insisted on reciting the *Aeneid* at the Circus dressed as Turnus—he was confused about the poem's ending, evidently.

Among the poets of Imperial Rome, Ovid deserves special mention for having fallen under Virgil's spell, so much so that the older poet became a source of inspiration for many of Ovid's works. Without Virgil's fictions, the most memorable passages of the *Metamorphoses* might not exist. Ovid borrowed many subjects from Virgil, including the myth of Orpheus and Eurydice as told in Book 4 of the *Georgics*, which he entirely recasts, turning it into an unforgettable story of unhappy love; direct reference to Virgil is made in lines 61-62 of Book 10. In the *Heroides*, Ovid completely rewrites, in an elegiac key, Dido's abandonment in Book 4 of the *Aeneid*. Compared to Virgil's version, Ovid's Dido appears more inclined to lamentation, agony, and victimhood as she pleads with her lover to stay in Carthage. Over the centuries, the queen, as Ovid imagines her, would become *the* literary stand-in for the wounded and abandoned lover. Whereas in Virgil, Dido does not refrain from insulting and cursing Aeneas—and for good reason.

Neither is there a dearth of parodies and satirical imitations of Virgil's work, the clearest indication of a success destined to leave a mark which would long inspire the envy of others. Among these is the diverting wit of one Numitorius, who twists the opening verse of the *Eclogues* like so: *Tityre, si toga calda tibi est, quo tegmina fagi?* Dear Tityrus, if it's hot under your toga, why hide behind a beech tree?

The humanist Scaligero hailed as interesting and entertaining the *Appendix Vergiliana*, a group of texts in a variety of meters written between the first century BC and the first century AD and printed as an appendix to editions of Virgil's works. Traditionally ascribed to the Mantuan poet himself—despite their unlikely authenticity—the *Appendix* demonstrates such a flair for subjects and stylistic ingenuity on the part of Virgil's earliest admirers as to make the poems of the so-called Epic Cycle—the sequels and prequels that followed on the heels of Homer and prolonged the stories of the protagonists of the *Iliad*—green with envy. The *Appendix* is made up of scientific subjects, country idylls, love poems, and pastoral parodies. Especially surprising are the invectives and insults of the Dirae, or "Curses," which prove that not all farmers in Cisalpine Gaul reacted to their land being confiscated with the composure of Tityrus and his friends.

After all the cloying encomiums and bland imitations of Virgil's work, the one person who seems to have taken to heart the true meaning of the *Aeneid* and the last wishes of the poet was Julius Hyginus, Augustus's librarian and the custodian of Virgil's original manuscripts—including the manuscript that the poet left unfinished at the time of his death. Asked, by virtue of his authority, to pronounce the last word on the poetic merits of the *Aeneid*, Hyginus refused to indulge his contemporaries in their pedantic debates and shut himself inside his library in the Temple of Apollo on the Palatine. Years later he stepped out of the temple with his review of the *Aeneid*, written in no fewer than five volumes, the *Commentarii in Vergilium*. In it, Hyginus pointed to the actual manuscripts to urge readers to pay attention to the authentic expression of the poet rather than amuse themselves by handing out Homeric trophies. Comparing the texts of the various codices, Hyginus corrected errors committed by the first amanuenses. More importantly, he could not ignore the human and artistic travails that had dogged Virgil as he wrote the epic, which, he argued, had to be considered unfinished, since they had been published against the author's will. But the voice of wise Hyginus went unheard, and his *Commentarii* was first unread and later lost; almost none of his texts have survived.

Between the principates of Vespasian and Domitian, the cult of Virgil had already given rise to solemn tributes on the Ides of October, the Mantuan poet's birthday, established by Silius Italicus, a crafty politician with thinly veiled artistic aspirations who went so far as to acquire Virgil's tomb in Naples. Meanwhile the first century of the new Christian era was coming to an end, and with it the first pagan—and explicitly Roman—phase of Virgil Fever.

What was about to begin was a long period of reading the *Aeneid* as an oracular text and worshipping its author as a Christian prophet.

* * *

As we get to the root of the old argument that Virgil was an *anima naturaliter christiana*, we have to acknowledge that not everyone who saw in his works a prophesy of the coming of Jesus Christ was a fanatic. We don't need a theology degree to remain at least a little taken in by the following lines from Book 4 of the *Eclogues*; a few Sunday school lessons should suffice.

> The final age the Sybil told has come and gone,
> and the great cycle of the centuries begins again:
> the Virgin now returns, and the reign of Saturn,
> and a new generation is descending from heaven.

Chaste Lucina, look with favor on this newborn child
by whom the Age of Iron will end and the golden age
arise around the world. Your own Apollo reigns.
(*Eclogues*, 4.4-10)

As early as the first century AD, while Rome was still
reeling from the advent of Christianity, there were those
who read these words and cried, "It's a miracle!" People
were quick to claim that these lines portended the Great
Year, which Plato describes in the *Timaeus* as a complete
cycle of planetary rotation and the return of the fixed stars
to their original position established by the demiurge,
which, according to some, would have taken place in Year
1, with the birth of Christ. However undeniable the simi-
larities may be—some details, like Virgil's use of the words
Virgo and *puer*, align extraordinarily well with Christian
doctrine—rational and philological explanations are no less
compelling.

Right after this, in line 11 of Eclogue 4, we read *te con-
sule*, "in your consulship," an explicit reference to Pollio,
a consul in 40 BC and close friend of Virgil and the unfortunate Cornelius Gallus. The child that the poet alludes to
here is Pollio's son, Asinius Gallus, whose life would come
to a tragic conclusion after a titillating affair with Agrippina.
I am well aware that it is not my place to judge. Yet in general my long immersion in classical texts, in the deafening
silence with which they are freighted, given the impossibil-
ity of our ever gaining access to documents, interviews, or
testimonials about their authors, has taught me to be less
severe and less cerebral when evaluating the interpretations

to which those authors have been subjected over the course of history; to spend less time trying to get inside the heads of classical writers, since we can never completely penetrate their minds, and more time putting myself in their shoes, which were firmly planted in the political and social moment in which they were read, because that *does* have a lot to tell us—via firsthand sources.

Though I have no intention of fueling conspiracy theories, neither do I feel like writing off as eccentric dupes those who, in the first centuries of the empire, thought they saw something religiously prophetic in Virgil's words and made the poet their beacon and guide. Of course, they were very naive and unscrupulous in their methods for believing they had read in Virgil's verses that which isn't written there, and in stubbornly ignoring that which they didn't want to see yet is clearly on the record. Still, they must have been desperate to place their faith in someone or something at a time when a thousand-year-old political story was about to end, that of Rome, having set in motion the fall of the Western Empire; and an entire human epoch, that of paganism, was being replaced by a new Christian era and all the mysticism and irrational fears that such a religion brought with it. More to the point, given the historic upheaval, with the world being knocked off its axis, the Romans would have believed in anything, and how can we blame them? It may as well have been Virgil, who offered plenty of reasons for people to get carried away with wild theories.

During the tumultuous centuries leading up to the collapse of the empire in 476, Virgil is turned into a saint—how else to characterize what happened—destined to spawn a faithful cult and the mass production of works celebrating him, not so different from the merchandising that has sprung up around the sanctuaries of Our Lady of Lourdes and Our Lady of Fátima. For starters, there was the proliferation of biographies of the Mantuan poet, whose life took on aspects of the divine that anticipated the hagiography of saints and martyrs. Virgil, a recluse who fiercely guarded his privacy, became the subject of legends, gossip, and miraculous tales, which had begun to multiply.

Chief among these was the fourth century *Life of Virgil* by the grammarian Aelius Donatus, who also deserves credit for standardizing the *Aeneid* adopted by schools during the Roman Empire. His biography, probably a transcription of the earlier *Life of Vergil* by Suetonius Tranquillus, Hadrian's private secretary, became the most read and studied during the Middle Ages and is still the main source of biographical details used by scholars today.

Four centuries after his death there was also a flurry of portraits made, whose authenticity is still the subject of debate among archaeologists. Still, it's nice to think we can glimpse the face of Virgil in the three portraits in the *Vergilius Romanus* codex mentioned earlier; or in the splendid mosaic rediscovered in Sousse and now on display at the Bardo National Museum of Tunis, which depicts the poet in a white tunic, surrounded by the Muses, holding the *Aeneid*. An excellent copy of the painting was later donated by the government of Tunisia to the Académie des Inscriptions et Belles-Lettres and exhibited at the 1900 Paris Exposition, while a stone's throw away the Eiffel Tower was being erected.

Special mention should be made of the "centos" of Virgil, collage texts composed of lines taken from the works of Virgil that quickly became their own literary genre. The genre takes its name from the Latin word *cento*, itself a derivation of the Greek κέντρων, meaning a garment made by stitching together different fabrics—a patchwork. Poems big and small, comprised of verses taken from the *Aeneid* out of context, multiplied exponentially, narrowing the modes of later poems, which obsessively adhered to Virgil's meter and language—at the very same time when Latin was losing currency and local varieties, which would soon give rise to the Romance languages, were ascendant. One person who helped consolidate literary Latin was the grammarian Macrobius, who considered Virgil the polestar of all classical Greco-Roman literature.

Many of these Virgilian centos have Christian content. It's worth remembering the *Cento Vergilianus de laudibus Christi*, which rearranged 694 of Virgil's lines to tell the story of the Old and New Testament and was "written" in the second half of the fourth century by a noblewoman, Faltonia Betitia Proba, the most influential Latin poet of Late Antiquity, and one of the rare women of letters whose name has come down to us. More than a thousand years later, in Paris, came *Sacra Aeneis*, or Sacred Aeneid, by Etienne de Pleure (1585-1635), canon of the Abbey of Saint-Victor, a cento which told the life of Christ with verses from Virgil's epic.

Maybe everybody knows how, after centuries of persecution and atrocities against the Christians, Emperor Constantine restored religious peace to the empire with his edict of Milan in 313 and granted religious freedom to all. Few, however, may be aware that Virgil played a role in the emperor's conversion to Catholicism. Though we do not know for sure whether the emperor suddenly swore off paganism because signs appeared to him during the Battle of the Milvian Bridge, as tradition would have it, or whether his choice was based on a political calculation, an *instrumentum regni* to restore civic peace in a dying Western empire torn apart by religious tensions, we do have proof that, in a famous speech to his followers (in the year 315, according to some), Constantine held forth on the prophecy of the *puer* contained in Eclogue 4.

From that moment on, bound to Christianity by imperial will, Virgil stopped being a poet. And became a symbol.

* * *

Virgil's cult status in Naples deserves a section all its own. The poet died in the city and was buried in the Parco Vergiliano a Piedigrotta, after supposedly dictating the famous epitaph carved on his tomb. The veneration of Virgil in Campania's capital had all the trappings of irrational idolatry and outrageous superstitions—which makes it a lot of fun to describe.

Named the second patron saint of the city, second only to the Parthenope Virgin—though he was clearly not a saint, he wasn't even consecrated!—Virgil, who went by Vergilius in the Late Middle Ages, was considered the spiritual protector of Naples, and legends and rituals that dabbled in magic and necromancy, and even involved the poor poet's bones, abounded. In fact, the more Christianity developed, and the more dogma and church hierarchy became organized, the more all the old pagan beliefs, by then celebrated by Catholics in a fashion as heterogenous as it was bizarre, centered on the figure of Virgil.

The tradition of attributing strange magical and healing powers to the poet seems to have begun in 1160, when an erudite Englishman named John of Salisbury wrote in one of his books that, during a sojourn in Naples, he had found proof that Virgil had liberated the city from a plague of flies after building a bronze statue of a fly that could affect the constellations. The poet was also credited with building a palladium, a model of Naples in a glass bottle, which had magical powers and had to be handled with the utmost care.

Amazing—shocking, really—is the catalog of seventeen miracles that the good Virgil conferred upon the city, recounted in the *Cronaca di Partenope* (or, *Croniche de la inclita Città de Napole*), a work by an unknown author operating at the court of King Robert of Anjou in the early 1300s. Browsing the book, you would think that Naples didn't even exist until Virgil came along: He is responsible for the walls and sewers, the streets and gates, the baths of Baia and Pozzuoli, and a medicinal garden. And then there is the strange crop of miracles involving animals: the construction of a stone fish that filled the Bay of Naples with aquatic life, of a gold leech that purified the city's wells, of a bronze horse that healed flesh-and-blood horses, as well as the invention of a strange copper cicada, which silenced the irritating chirrup of insects at night, and, combined with a statue that could summon favorable winds, guaranteed Naples the breeze that the poet sang about in his own time.

One enduring legend claimed that Virgil had blessed an ostrich egg kept, like a talisman, in the foundations of the Castel dell'Ovo (i.e., the Castle of the Egg).

But Virgil and Naples' happy union was doomed, just like all stories that are too good to be true—especially when the stories have zero basis in reality. Envious parties—the Norman conquerors specifically, with the support of the Church—did not hesitate to attack the remains of Virgil.

At the end of the 1200s, various stories get conflated and two different legends emerge. According to the first, Virgil's palladium was cracked, a bad omen. The other is far more macabre. Apparently, another English scholar, known only by his first name, Ludowicus, stole the remains of Virgil from the tomb of Piedigrotta in the hopes of weakening defenses in Naples and handing the city over to the Normans. Later, the bones of the poet were recovered and guarded in the Castel dell'Ovo before being permanently lost. According to another version, recounted in the *Otia imperialia* by Gervase of Tilbury, a professor in Bologna and Marshal of the Kingdom of Arles, this same Englishman, whom no one knew yet everyone said was highly intelligent, broke into Virgil's tomb, found the body of the poet perfectly preserved, and carried off the book of magic lying underneath his head.

However it happened, at the start of the 1300s Virgil no longer blessed Naples with his incredible medieval miracles. But he didn't entirely vanish from city lore—still alive and well to this day—and superstitions, which the legends of Virgil may actually have helped give rise to. Once a glimmer of reason returned, in the 1700s, classicists set to interrogating the inexplicable reasons that led Naples to turn the poet into a magician, seeing as neither the *Aeneid* nor the *Eclogues* nor the *Georgics* make mention of secret spells or wizardry.

One interesting, though unproven, theory is that it stemmed from a simple mix-up of names: The supernatural works by another Virgil, an Arab illusionist and philosopher, which were translated into Latin and disseminated to the rest of the Western world from Toledo, were attributed to Virgil the Latin poet. Even if the causes remain unknown, what is certain is that the extraordinary stories about the poet—talismans, white magic, precious metals capable of changing into other elements—are imbued with details that directly correspond to the secret science of alchemy, which in those years was spreading throughout Europe thanks to translations from Arabic of works of esoteric and occult philosophy.

Hence Virgil earned yet another epithet; after having been called a court poet, a soothsayer, a saint and a seer, Virgil next became, through no fault of his own, an alchemist.

Virgil from Dante to Our Day

You can't talk about the *Divine Comedy* without talking about the *Aeneid*.

And it's impossible to peruse Virgil's epic without being

put in mind of Dante Alighieri, who modeled his work on the Mantuan poet and made him his literary guide in the Underworld. Virgil's shade introduces himself in the first canto of the *Inferno* (vv. 67-75), recounting his life to a speechless Dante, who has just lost his way in the dark wood:

> . . . Not man, I was once a man.
> Both of my parents came from Lombardy
> and both were native Mantuans.
>
> And I was born *sub Julio,* though late,
> and lived in Rome under the good Augustus
> during the time of false and lying gods.
>
> I was a poet and I sang about the just
> son of Anchises who came from Troy
> when fires destroyed the pride of Ilium.

With reverence and embarrassment—"with shame upon his brow"—Dante asks for help from the shade of the man he considers his "master and author," the "honor and light" of all poets who came after him, whose *Aeneid* Dante had learned by "long study and great love." This is how they begin their journey to the afterlife, during which Virgil will be a constant presence and trusted (human and literary) guide until the very end of Canto 30 of the *Purgatory*, when Dante turns to find the spirit of the poet has vanished and been replaced by Beatrice. Elsewhere in this book, in our discussion of Book 6 of the *Aeneid*, we have mentioned how much the *Commedia*—and therefore all Italian literature post-Dante—is indebted to Virgil's epic, especially in its depictions of hell and demons and bolgias.

In Canto 21 of the *Purgatory*, Dante acknowledges the specific debt he owes the *Aeneid* with the most beautiful of metaphors: a mother metaphor. The following words are addressed to Virgil by Statius, a Roman poet in the age of Flavian:

> I speak of the *Aeneid*, which was to me
> a mother and a nurse as I wrote my verses:
> my work would weigh nothing without it.
> (*Purgatory*, 21.97-99)

Scholars have calculated that, from Cerberus to Charon, from the Harpies to Pier delle Vigne, throughout Limbo and its cast of ancient authors, direct reference is made to the *Aeneid* over three hundred times in the *Divine Comedy*. Not to mention that it gave him the idea for the journey to the Underworld and is responsible for the restrained, restless tone and atmosphere of the story.

More than the allusions and (some more, some less indirect) quotations, what makes Dante's borrowings significant is the unprecedented respect they show Virgil, who is finally appreciated as a classical poet and whose work is extolled as invaluable. After nearly a millennium in which all that was taught about the author of the *Aeneid* was his role as a Christian prophet—a role foisted on him—and his supposed magical powers, with no consideration for the significance of his verses, Dante finally restores Virgil's poetry to its rightful place as a central text to be studied.

Dante is not only interested in asking Virgil "how a man makes himself eternal." More than anything, he wants Virgil to teach him how to make immortal poetry. It is thanks to the *Commedia* that later authors take a serious interest in the *Aeneid* as a masterpiece of expressive language and narrative craftsmanship, dispelling centuries of legends and rigid rhetorical rules for "writing like Virgil" without ever having really read Virgil. Saint Augustine called such deadening academic exercises all smoke and wind.

Add to that the imaginary world created by the *Aeneid* and sublimated into Dante's *Comedy*, at a time when no one in Europe knew Greek and the term "classic" practically stood for Virgil. The incarnations of classical heroes and heroines were Aeneas, not Achilles or Ulysses; Rome, not Ithaca; Dido, not Helen; Ascanius, not Telemachus; Turnus, not Paris. And it was from them that new stories were spun.

Ancient myths, onomastics, geography, art, and bits of science drew on the works of Virgil and not—even if Dante calls him the "sovereign poet"—the works of Homer, which no one could read. Painters, poets, musicians, architects, and artists of all kinds would copy them throughout the Middle Ages until the advent of Humanism.

Of course, Dante did have to navigate Virgil's paganism. No matter how pious or illuminated, Virgil was born "during the time of false and lying gods" and by force of circumstance had never been baptized. It would have been inconceivable for medieval man to grant salvation to anyone born before Christ and excluded from the light of faith. In the *Commedia,* Limbo is the eternal station of the unbaptized, the eternal "mourning" place. There, the virtuous pagans join children who died prematurely in their insatiable thirst for the divine.

That is the condition of Virgil, who cannot take Dante through paradise, as once again Statius expresses in a famous tercet (which happens to be followed by a reference to the Christian reading of eclogue 4):

> You did as one who goes in darkness,
> bearing the light behind him, not profiting himself,
> but making those who follow after wise.
> (*Purgatory*, 22.67-69)

In Dante's *Divine Comedy*, Virgil is forced to walk in the dark, carrying a torch that does not illuminate the road ahead of him, but casts a light for those who come after him. Perhaps, in the 1300s, the Mantuan poet's personal journey and artistic travails still lay in shadow, but a new light had been lit, one that would clarify the *Aeneid*, banish superstition, and light the way for philology, which was about to emerge with the dawn of Humanism.

* * *

Humanism made the classics central to people's vision of life and art again, and, alongside Cicero, Virgil became the most widely read author. His *Aeneid*, which advocated for pietas and honesty, became the most beloved epic, as well as an enduring model for all poets. Before humanism, Petrarch had been so intensely drawn to the moral dignity and veiled melancholy of Virgil's characters (the first reference to style in the *Canzoniere* is to the formal perfection of the *Aeneid*), that he commissioned his friend, the painter Simone Martini, then at the court of Avignon, to make him a magnificent miniature for his personal copy of Servius' *Commentary on Virgil*, now held at the Ambrosian Library in Milan.

The first Humanists were not only intrigued by the large number of illuminated manuscripts of the *Aeneid* then circulating in Europe, which they set to work printing and teaching from; they were also in thrall to the delicacy of Virgil's poetry. Inspired by the *Eclogues*, Giovanni Pontano composed his elegant *Naeniae,* a collection of poems and lullabies written for his son. In addition to writing two pastoral works, *Manto* and *Rusticus*, the scholar and poet Poliziano retold the "fabula" of Orpheus and Eurydice. And Jacopo Sannazzaro, known as the Christian Virgil for the elegance of his verses, composed *Arcadia*, a bucolic poem with Virgilian echoes.

The Late Renaissance, which saw the rebirth of the epic and the affirmation of vernacular speech as worthy of literature, cemented Virgil's reputation. Ludovico Ariosto, first, and Torquato Tasso, later, would make the characters of the *Aeneid* once again thrum with humanity, in tales of intense battles and tender loves. In Ariosto's *Orlando Furioso*, Cloridano and Medoro mirror the innocent and organic gestures of Nisus and Euryalus, celebrating the value of friendship, while the beautiful Angelica is shrouded in a Virgilian aura of peace and serenity. Tasso begins his *Gerusalemme Liberata*, "I sing of pious armies and the captain," almost a paraphrase of the opening of the *Aeneid,* demonstrating why Tasso's poem is called the most Virgilian of Italian epics. Likewise, the pride of his character Clorinda is modeled on Virgil's heroic virgin Camilla, and in the mystery of Armida we can spy Dido's combination of love and grief.

Virgil's fortunes were eclipsed when the Age of Reason turned on the lights in Europe. Beginning in the eighteenth century, the *Aeneid* appeared too "fantastical," too mythic, inadequate to the rational and scientific pretexts of the Enlightenment. Aside from its plot, deemed far-fetched and out of step with the new critical impulse of the day, there were many reasons why writers and scholars distanced themselves from the poem.

Virgil was still encumbered by legends and superstitions that proved hard to shed, and the specter of Augustan propaganda began to undermine the poem's reputation. The circumstances surrounding the *Aeneid*'s dissemination attracted far fewer scholars of philology, a discipline that was just then gaining prestige and adapting its inquiries to the scientific method. The fortunes of Virgilian manuscripts had been, over the centuries, far less perilous than those of Homer's codices, and people began to attribute the vast quantity of them to the political will of the Roman Empire, which they believed made the poem a kind of educational manifesto.

In the 1800s, one of Virgil's greatest detractors was Giacomo Leopardi, who pulled no punches in the *Zibaldone*, harshly criticizing the *Aeneid* and preferring the *Iliad* and *Odyssey.* (The poet of Recanati did, however, know his Virgil, having studied his verses all his life.) In both the *Operette morali* and the *Zibaldone*, Leopardi dismisses Virgil as mediocre and is perplexed by his success compared to other "more talented" Latin authors, like Lucan. The unmerited recognition of the *Aeneid* had to be attributed, he believed, to the crude tastes of readers who prefer their beauty "broad and obvious" rather than "subtle and implied." Leave it to death to put an end to the literary enmity between the two greatest poets Italy has ever known: The remains of Giacomo Leopardi lie not far from the tomb of Virgil, in the Parco di Piedigrotta in Naples.

While in France Virgil won the admiration of Victor Hugo, Charles Baudelaire, and Louis Aragon, and in 1923 the Sorbonne organized a stately tribute in the poet's honor, in Italy, Fascism cast a dark shadow over the *Aeneid*, and the poem has yet to get out from under the regime's grubby commentaries and intellectual dishonesty. Virgil emerged from the Second World War badly bruised by the manipulation of the Fascists and the total excoriation of Simone Weil. Yet he also bore a new voice, intimate and weathered, as people attempted to find words to describe the dramatic moment. That voice belonged to Hermann Broch, an Austrian writer and naturalized citizen of the United States, who, in his novel *The Death of Virgil*, first published in 1945 and in Italy in 1962, imagines the poet's final days as he journeyed from Greece to Rome, lamenting his failure to finish the *Aeneid*. "The immeasurable meaning of life only springs from the perfect fullness of meaning revealed by death," writes Broch in his five-hundred-page tome, in which he tries, by recounting the death of Virgil, to make sense of the grief of an entire era.

In 1949, Giorgio Caproni claimed to see in Aeneas the condition of contemporary man, his loneliness and scandalous grief. Despite this condition, the hero neither gives up nor gives ground—the way of Aeneas is to get back up and rebuild.

I have decided to end this book with a few lines from Caproni's poem about the relevance of the *Aeneid*—its urgency, rather, for Aeneas has once again begun his passage from life before to life after, and we with him, determined and uncertain.

> In the racing heart of your Aeneas,
> alone in the catastrophe, his bony foot
> covered with blisters, the coast ablaze
> with red smoke—Aeneas, who tries
> in vain to carry the wreck of the past
> to safety as a drumbeat beats
> the tottering walls, who grips the hand
> of a future too weak to stand up straight,
> who makes his sad flight across a beach
> still hot with blood. What kind of escape
> can the sea provide you (green
> moth of white beacons) if you, like him,
> shudder at the thought you've reached
> the point of total solitude, more
> determined and uncertain than our dark years?

ACKNOWLEDGMENTS

There is a form of despair,
folly, *une folie, ma chére,*
a form of despair that
we will not stop
not you or me or blessed books
or iron erudition   ·
(ignore the fact
that the author himself
is a poor ignoramus)
a dry despair, white
as the early October moon
in the northern wind
a despair of fast fixed colors that know no reason
that cannot be put under a spell
or dispelled.
—GIORGIO MANGANELLI, from *Poems*

At the start of each chapter, the reader will find excerpts from the poems of Giorgio Manganelli. They have been a great source of inspiration and comfort, since I undertook the pivotal research that led to the creation of this book during weeks spent sheltering in place at my home in Paris due to the restrictions imposed by the Covid-19 epidemic.

My decision to include them here is based on what I saw as Manganelli's kinship with the frank despair of Virgil in the *Aeneid*, and with the tenacity of poetry as a means of affirmation and redress, despite the obvious differences between the writers in terms of historical age, style and ambition.

I discovered Manganelli's sharp, almost caustic poetry while reading Sandro Veronesi's 2019 novel *The Hummingbird*. When the character Luisa sends three of the Milanese writer's poems to the novel's protagonist, Marco Carrera, she adds, "I have just realized that I will never be through with Giorgio Manganelli."

Sincere thanks to Crocetti, the publisher, for the care and respect with which they posthumously edited and published the poems with the help of the author's daughter, Lietta Manganelli. Thanks, also, for not hesitating to email me a PDF of the text one Sunday evening in March, when all the libraries in Europe were closed, without asking any questions not already implicitly answered by my urgent need to read Manganelli.

The Latin dictionary I consulted was the *Dictionnaire latin-français* by F. Gaffiot, published by Hachette, though I only had access to the abridged version online. For weeks, I was unable to get my hands on my Castiglioni-Mariotti, a dictionary that I had consulted since high school, as worn as it was beloved, because I lost it during my latest— last—move. Thanks to the website lexilogos.com and the generosity of its creators—from "a cove in Provence"—for making available the only tools that enrich those who interrogate them: dictionaries.

The reference book I used for background research in Latin literature was Antonio La Penna's precious *Prima lezione di letteratura latina* (Rome-Bari: Laterza, 2003). The two textbooks for high school students that I consulted were *Nati per leggere. Mito ed epica* (Milan: Bruno Mondadori, 2012) and *Il mito e l'epica* (Turin: Paravia, 2018). Warm thanks to Monica Volpe, literature teacher at the Instituto Comprensivo Palombara Sabina, for her friendship and for having procured these books for me.

I wish to thank my dear editor, Giovanni Carletti, for once again placing his trust in me. Without our conversations this book might never have come to be and certainly would never have become what it is. Thanks, too, to my literary agent, Carmen Prestia, a model of professionalism for women everywhere.

I owe the idea of arranging and ordering the chapters as I have to André Aciman, whom I wish to thank for reading the manuscript and more importantly for being my friend.

Finally, thanks to two people without whom this book would not exist:

One evening, in the heart of Rome, with the city all lit up for the Christmas holiday, I subjected my closest friend, Alberto Cattaneo, to my ideas for my next book—a book I had yet to write let alone think through. All of my ideas were muddled and sketchy, yet he still believed in my plan to write a book about the *Aeneid*. Thanks to him, I began to believe in it too. Thanks, Alberto, every book I've written is your doing. You are the one person who has endured—more tenacious than Aeneas—in the acknowledgments of all my books and in my affections.

During the long weeks of lockdown in Montmartre, no one was better company than my friend and French translator Béatrice Robert-Boissier. Her friendship, her refinement, her elegance, her wit and her talent have been a constant source of inspiration and encouragement. Thank you for being by my side as I wrote this book, from the first word to the last. And thanks for giving me the means to do it at a time when I was unable to procure the physical books I needed for this study and consult hardcopy sources that weren't already in my studio apartment. If I was able to access online archives, dictionaries and digital catalogs, I owe it to you and you alone, to your professionalism and your precious and shrewd advice. Thanks for putting up with me; not everyone wants to spend a pandemic listening to someone talk about Aeneas every day.

Lest I forget: For all the haters out there, thanks, as always, to my dog.

TRANSLATOR'S NOTE

The Italian edition includes bibliographical notes on Italian translations of the classics quoted or consulted by the author. Along with the Italian translations of Virgil by Guido Paduano, I have consulted Robert Fagles's *The Aeneid* (London: Penguin Books, 2008); David Ferry's *The Eclogues of Virgil* (New York: FSG, 1999), *The Georgics of Virgil* (New York: FSG, 2006) and *The Aeneid* (Chicago: University of Chicago Press, 2017); and John Dryden's seventeenth-century translation of Virgil's epic. For their translations of Dante, I am indebted to Robert and Jean Hollander and Henry Wadsworth Longfellow.

THE *AENEID*: A BRIEF SUMMARY

BOOK 1

After seven long years at sea, Aeneas and his companions are swept to the coast of Africa by a violent storm unleashed by Juno. There, the exiles are warmly welcomed by Dido, the queen of Carthage, who serves them a lavish feast and pleads with Aeneas to tell the story of their trials.

BOOK 2

Aeneas describes how Troy is taken in by Ulysses's wooden horse. As Troy burns, Fate compels him to flee his native city and found a country where he can set down the household gods given to him by Hector. Joining him on his journey are his young son Ascanius and his infirm father Anchises, but his wife Creusa inexplicably vanishes in the flames.

BOOK 3

Aeneas continues to tell the story of the Trojan refugees' harrowing voyage and their stops in Thrace, Delos, Crete, and the Strophades, islands haunted by Harpies, creatures with human faces and avian bodies. Next they travel to Epirus, where Aeneas meets Hector's wife Andromache, and Sicily, where, near Trapani, Anchises dies of old age. Finally, their fatal shipwreck leads the exiles to the court of Dido.

BOOK 4
Venus sends her son Cupid to Carthage to make the queen fall in love with Aeneas. The two lie together in a cave during a storm and their ensuing affair makes Aeneas forget everything, even the will of Fate. Months later Aeneas comes to his senses and prepares his fleet to sail for Latium. After a vicious fight with Aeneas, Dido throws herself on the sword of the man she loves. Before dying, she swears that Carthage and Rome shall from then on be sworn enemies.

BOOK 5
The Trojans depart Carthage and land in Sicily again, where they perform games in honor of Anchises. Juno attempts to destroy their ships, but a rain of gold puts out the fire. The eldest refugees refuse to go on and set up a small city, while Aeneas and his loyal companions set sail for Latium. During their voyage, Misenus is abducted by Sleep and disappears at sea.

BOOK 6
Having reached Cumae, Aeneas climbs up to the Temple of Apollo, where the Sibyl escorts him on his descent to the Underworld. Bearing a golden bough for Proserpine, Aeneas crosses into Hades and reaches the river guarded by Charon. On the shores of the river, he encounters many

souls, including those of his friend Deiphobus, who had fallen at Troy; the unlucky helmsman Palinurus; and Dido, who reacts with anger at the sight of the man she loved. Finally, Aeneas is reunited with his father in the Elysian Fields. Anchises tells him of the glorious future that awaits Rome thanks to the lineage of his son, which will eventually produce Romulus and, centuries on, Augustus.

BOOK 7

At the mouth of the Tiber Aeneas recognizes Latium as the homeland foretold by Fate. The Trojans seek the hospitality of King Latinus, who graciously welcomes the exiles and offers his daughter Lavinia to Aeneas. But Juno stokes the hatred of Latinus's wife Amanta, and Amanta, in turn, incites brave Turnus, Lavinia's betrothed, to take up arms against Aeneas.

BOOK 8

With war in Latium imminent, a hard-pressed Aeneas is aided by King Evander, the founder of Pallantion, who puts at Aeneas's disposal an army led by his young son Pallas. Meanwhile Venus gives Aeneas a shield forged by Vulcan that depicts the history of Rome, all the way up to the Battle of Actium in which Octavian defeated Antony and Cleopatra.

BOOK 9

The war in Latium begins. A pair of young friends, Euryalus and Nisus, are brutally murdered by Turnus. Turnus desecrates their bodies and manages to penetrate the Trojan camp, but he is given chase and saves himself by jumping into the Tiber.

Book 10
Though Aeneas regains the upper hand in the battle, Turnus viciously kills young Pallas. Aeneas avenges Pallas by killing the Latin Mezentius.

Book 11
A truce is established so the two sides can bury their dead. The battle resumes, this time with Camilla, the virgin queen of the Volscians, who kills many Trojans before falling in battle.

Book 12
Despite knowing Fate is not on his side, Turnus challenges Aeneas to a duel. The Trojan gets the better of him and is about to spare Turnus's life when he notices the sword-belt that belonged to Pallas. Aeneas takes vengeance on Turnus, stabbing him to death. Turnus's soul flees indignantly to the shades.

Who Was Aeneas?

Son of the mortal Anchises and the goddess Venus, Aeneas is the prince of the Dardanians, one of the Illyrian tribes in Dardania, an ancient region of the Balkans. In the *Iliad* Homer describes Aeneas as a brave warrior and an ally of the Trojans during the Trojan War, given his marriage to Priam's daughter Creusa. His long search for a new homeland after the fall of Troy is recounted by Virgil in the *Aeneid*. After various misadventures and a stopover in Carthage as a guest of Queen Dido, Aeneas lands in Latium where he sows the seeds of the Roman Empire.

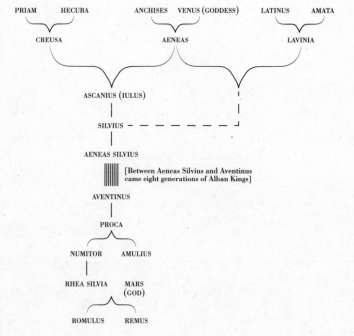

ABOUT THE AUTHOR

Andrea Marcolongo is an Italian journalist, writer, Classics scholar, and former speech writer for Prime Minister Matteo Renzi. Her book on Greek, *The Ingenious Language* (Europa, 2019), was an international bestseller. She is also the author of *The Heroic Measure*. She lives in Paris, France.